NEW STUDIES IN BIBLICAL THEOLOGY

D. A. Carson, Series Editor

NEW STUDIES IN BIBLICAL THEOLOGY

Possessed by God
DAVID PETERSON

Whoredom
RAYMOND C. ORTLUND, JR.

Jesus and the Logic of History
PAUL W. BARNETT

Hear, My Son
DANIEL J. ESTES

Jesus and the Logic of History

Paul W. Barnett

WILLIAM B. EERDMANS PUBLISHING COMPANY
GRAND RAPIDS, MICHIGAN / CAMBRIDGE, U.K.

© 1997 Paul W. Barnett

Published 1997 in the U.K. by
APOLLOS (an imprint of Inter-Varsity Press)
and in the United States of America by
Wm. B. Eerdmans Publishing Co.
255 Jefferson Ave. S.E., Grand Rapids, Michigan 49503 /
P.O. Box 163, Cambridge CB3 9PU U.K.
All rights reserved

Printed in the United States of America

01 00 99 98 97   7 6 5 4 3 2 1

ISBN 0-8028-4410-3 (pbk. : alk. paper)

For
Bill Haffenden,
paraklētos

Contents

Series preface

New Studies in Biblical Theology is a series of monographs that address key issues in the discipline of biblical theology. Contributions to the series focus on one or more of three areas: 1. the nature and status of biblical theology, including its relations with other disciplines (*e.g.* historical theology, exegesis, systematic theology, historical criticism, narrative theology); 2. the articulation and exposition of the structure of thought of a particular biblical writer or corpus; and 3. the delineation of a biblical theme across all or part of the biblical corpora.

Above all, these monographs are creative attempts to help thinking Christians understand their Bibles better. The series aims simultaneously to instruct and to edify, to interact with the current literature, and to point the way ahead. In God's universe, mind and heart should not be divorced: in this series we will try not to separate what God has joined together. While the footnotes interact with the best of the scholarly literature, the text is uncluttered with untransliterated Greek and Hebrew, and tries to avoid too much technical jargon. The volumes are written within the framework of confessional evangelicalism, but there is always an attempt at thoughtful engagement with the sweep of the relevant literature.

This volume interacts thoughtfully and tellingly with the literature of the 'third questers'. Dr Barnett offers important contributions to the manner in which we may responsibly work as both historians and theologians to understand not only the nascent Christian church, but also the historical Jesus whom they confessed. This study yields fresh insight not only into Paul's thought, but also into the relationship between Paul and Jesus. Dr Barnett's work deserves wide dissemination.

D. A. Carson
Trinity Evangelical Divinity School, Deerfield, Illinois

Author's preface

Christianity is a historical religion in at least two senses. It is historical in the sense that it has been continuously part of world history for a long time. Indeed, much of the world community still reckons its years from and before the birth of Christ. Christianity is also historical because Jesus was a real man who was born, lived and died at a particular time and place. This can be demonstrated for him by the same methodology – and just as easily – as for the emperor Tiberius, in whose era and empire Jesus became a public figure. Similarly, the rise and spread of earliest Christianity are demonstrably factual. The origins of Christianity are not mythical in character.

While there have been times in the past when mythical origins have been proposed, this is not the current view. Rather, at this time a significant body of scholars are redefining Jesus *historically*. There is a presumption that he cannot have been a supernatural figure, the God-man of the church's creeds, and that he must be capable of other explanations. It is those other explanations which have come into prominence in the final quarter of the twentieth century. In a sense the manifold reconstructions reflect the deconstructionist, individualist character of our postmodern era. There are as many Jesuses as there are people who write about him.

It is the argument of this book that the 'logic' of history demands a Jesus who is definable and about whom a practical consensus can be reached. By this 'logic' it is argued that the Christ of the early church's faith and proclamation must have borne a close relationship to Jesus the historical figure.

This book arose out of the Moore Theological College Annual Lectures (1996), which were also entitled *Jesus and the Logic of History*. The opportunity to reflect on this critical subject was provided by the kind invitation to the lectureship extended by the Principal of Moore College, Dr Peter Jensen. I thank the

Faculty and students for their attention and questions. I am deeply grateful to Dr Peter Head, of Oak Hill College, London, who offered many helpful suggestions and criticisms.

Paul Barnett

Abbreviations

ANRW	*Austieg und Niedergang der römischen Welt*
BAR	*Biblical Archaeological Review*
BBR	*Bulletin for Biblical Research*
Bib	*Biblica*
BJRL	*Bulletin of the John Rylands Library*
BR	*Biblical Review*
CBQ	*Catholic Biblical Quarterly*
CH	*Church History*
DJG	*Dictionary of Jesus and the Gospels,* ed. J. B. Green, S. McKnight and I. H. Marshall (Downers Grove and Leicester: IVP, 1992)
DPL	*Dictionary of Paul and his Letters,* ed. R. P. Martin, G. F. Hawthorne, D. G. Reid (Downers Grove and Leicester: IVP, 1993)
EDNT	*Exegetical Dictionary of the New Testament,* ed. H. Balz and G. Schneider, 3 vols. (T. and T. Clark, 1990–93).
ExpT	*Expository Times*
HJ	*Heythrop Journal*
HTR	*Harvard Theological Review*
JBL	*Journal of Biblical Literature*
JQR	*Jewish Quarterly Review*
JSNT	*Journal for the Study of the New Testament*
JSOT	*Journal for the Study of the Old Testament*
JTS	*Journal of Theological Studies*
NovT	*Novum Testamentum*
NTS	*New Testament Studies*
RTR	*Reformed Theological Review*
SJT	*Scottish Journal of Theology*
SNTS	*Society for New Testament Studies*
SP	*Studia Patristica*
TB	*Tyndale Bulletin*
TDNT	*Theological Dictionary of the New Testament,* ed. G. Kittel

and G. Friedrich, trans. and ed. G. W. Bromiley, 10 vols. (Grand Rapids: Eerdmans, 1946–76)

ThT   *Theology Today*
TJ   *Trinity Journal*
USQR *Union Seminary Quarterly Review*

Chapter One
Jesus and the practice of history

Introduction

Christianity is currently facing one of its most profound challenges, one that cuts to its heart. Between 1980 and 1992 there were published no fewer than 260 books, articles and reviews devoted to life-of-Jesus studies.[1] The challenge is that for the most part, this volume of literature presents a Jesus who is unrecognizable to the Christian faith as expressed in the historic creeds and confessions of the church.

For the greater part of the twentieth century, scholars have been sceptical about the recoverability of the historical Jesus. In these last decades, however, the pendulum has swung to the opposite extreme. In 1971 Leander Keck could comment that '"the search for the real Jesus" is a dead-end street'. By 1988, however, Marcus Borg could refer to a 'renaissance' in Jesus studies, noting that 'we can . . . know as much about Jesus as . . . about any figure in the ancient world'.[2] (Such confidence stands in contrast with Bultmann's famous remark of 1926 that 'we can know almost nothing concerning the life and personality of Jesus'.) 'Renaissance' is no exaggeration. The body of literature includes some very substantial texts, by such authors as Vermes

---

[1] For useful surveys of this literature see B. Witherington, *The Jesus Quest* (Downers Grove: IVP, 1995); C. A. Evans, *Jesus* (Grand Rapids: Baker, 1992); W. R. Telford, 'Major Trends and Interpretative Issues in the Study of Jesus', in *Studying the Historical Jesus*, ed. B. Chilton and C. A. Evans (Leiden: Brill, 1994); G. R. Elton, *The Practice of History* (Sydney: Sydney University Press, 1967); N. T. Wright, 'Quest for the Historical Jesus', in *Anchor Bible Dictionary* 3 (Garden City, NY: Doubleday, 1992), pp. 796–802. The Jesus Seminar is critically reviewed in various articles in *Jesus Under Fire*, ed. J. Wilkins and P. Moreland (Grand Rapids: Zondervan, 1995); see especially pp. 1–99.

[2] L. E. Keck, *A Future for the Historical Jesus* (Nashville: Abingdon, 1971), p. 9; M. Borg, *Jesus: A New Vision* (San Francisco: Harper and Row, 1988), p. 15; *idem*, 'A Renaissance in Jesus Studies', *ThT* 45 (1988), pp. 280–292.

(a trilogy), E. P. Sanders, Charlesworth, Crossan and Meier (a trilogy). Moreover, there have been ongoing specialist study groups such as the Society of Biblical Literature Historical Jesus Section and the widely publicized Jesus Seminar. Inevitably this flood of scholarly work has overflowed through the electronic and print media to the general public. Jesus has been the subject of cover stories in international journals, popular television programmes, and a number of best-selling pseudo-academic literary reconstructions.

What has emerged from this plethora of research? In the main, the scholars make a point of asserting Jesus' Jewishness, as reflected in such titles as *Jesus the Jew* (Vermes), *Jesus and Judaism* (Sanders), *Jesus' Jewishness* (Charlesworth) and *A Marginal Jew* (Meier), to take a few examples.[3] A minority of the scholars, however, emphasize Jesus' Hellenistic environment above the Judaic. Here Jesus emerges as a teacher in the Cynic tradition (Downing, Mack, Crossan). These scholars tend to be quite selective in their use of sources, preferring the so-called 'Q' source and the *Gospel of Thomas* to the four canonical gospels.

What kind of Jesus is to be found in these works? If the miracle tradition in the gospels is the focus, Jesus emerges as healer and exorcist (Vermes). Where the sayings are regarded as central, Jesus is seen as teacher. Depending on whether the sayings concentrated on are aphorisms, proverbs or apocalypticisms, Jesus is a sage (Downing), a subversive sage (Borg) or an eschatological prophet (Sanders, Charlesworth). Where the Son of man sayings are viewed as primary, Jesus is seen as a social prophet (Horsley). If a particular social context for Jesus is suggested, his profile is sharpened. A group, class or activity for Jesus is sought, or perhaps even a sub-class, adding to the

---

[3] The issue of the Jewishness of Jesus has been addressed from both a historical and a theological perspective. D. J. Harrington, 'The Jewishness of Jesus: Facing Some Problems', *CBQ* 49 (1987), pp. 1–13, sets out some of the historical problems arising from the growing knowledge of Jesus' Jewish background. The more we know of its diversity, the more difficult it is to locate Jesus within it. B. Hebblethwaite, 'The Jewishness of Jesus from the Perspectives of Christian Doctrine', *SJT* 42 (1989), pp. 27–44, seeks to reinstate the fact of Jesus' Jewishness into the matrix of theology, the theology of the incarnation and the theology, based on fact, of the resurrection. Otherwise Jesus is not capable of sustaining Christianity. B. Witherington, *Jesus the Sage* (Edinburgh: T. and T. Clark, 1994), pp. 147–208, locates Jesus within the tradition of Jewish wisdom teachers.

plurality and complexity of the analyses. Where the Jewish rabbinic context is emphasized, Jesus emerges as a rabbi (Chilton) or, more specifically, a Pharisee (Falk). Where apocalyptic Judaism is seen as his milieu, he is, for example, a humane apocalyptist (Charlesworth) or a reasonable visionary (Sanders). The variations of definition arising from these methodologies have prompted the social commentator Paul Johnson, though not a specialist in the field, to observe shrewdly that 'using the same texts and scholarly apparatus, dozens, perhaps hundreds of different Jesuses can be constructed'.[4]

It is an interesting coincidence that the closing decades of the nineteenth century also witnessed a spate of books on Jesus, many of them idealistic and romantic in character, reflecting the spirit of that age. The current Jesus reconstructions are also idealistic, but are shaped more by the values of late-second-millennium political correctness. The Jesus of the 'third questers', as they are called, often looks remarkably like the scholars who write about him: postmodern, ideologically reformist and eminently reasonable.

In the late nineteenth century, Martin Kähler wrote against the numerous 'lives of Jesus', making the famous distinction between the 'so-called Jesus of history' and the 'Christ of faith'. Kähler's book repays careful reading. The distinction he made, the issues he raised and the criticisms he offered come across with freshness and great power despite the intervening years. Kähler argued that modern scholars cannot create a 'fifth' gospel via their own biographical efforts; saving faith can arise only from the proclamation of the exalted Christ, who fulfils the prophets, and who is to be found in the whole New Testament. His sharp words for such biographers have application to those who engage in Jesus reconstructions now. 'What is usually happening', he wrote, 'is that the image of Jesus is being refracted through the spirit of these gentlemen.'[5]

The argument of Kähler's book, which is historically rather than theologically based, none the less has profound implications for theology, and for Christology in particular. The uniqueness of Christ is challenged implicitly or explicitly by the

---

[4] *Daily Telegraph*, 13 September 1992.
[5] M. Kähler, *The So-Called Historical Jesus and the Historic Biblical Christ* (Philadelphia: Fortress, 1964), p. 57.

great majority of recent historical works devoted to Jesus. Note the words of E. P. Sanders: 'I do not doubt that in some ways . . . Jesus was unique; in some ways everybody is unique . . . In fact we cannot say that a single one of the things known about Jesus was unique.'[6] Sanders's remark bears on the relationship between history and theology. The Christ of the church's faith and proclamation rests on the Jesus of history, Jesus as he was, historically speaking. But if the historical Jesus is undercut and reduced in stature and being, so too, in consequence, is the Christ of faith. Thus the practice and method of history are not irrelevant to the practice and method of theology. Christ's incarnation occurred in time and space, that is, in history. The practice and method of history are related to the practice and method of theology.

The practice and method of history

The work of life-of-Jesus scholars purports to arise out of historical enquiry and so raises questions which go to the heart of the practice and method of history.

History defined

'History', wrote the Tudor historian G. R. Elton, 'deals with events, not states; it investigates things that happen and not things that are.' Its concern is for 'the transformation of things (people, institutions, ideas and so on) from one state into another'.[7] History, therefore, may be defined as 'those human sayings, thoughts, deeds and sufferings which occurred in the past and have left a present deposit; and it deals with them from the point of view of happening, change and the particular'.[8] In short, history so defined deals with phenomena, and, where possible, seeks to explain them.

This understanding of history appears to have informed the thinking of C. F. D. Moule in his important work, *The Phenomenon of the New Testament*.[9] Moule referred to 'the coming

[6] *Jesus and Judaism* (London: SCM, 1984), p. 240.

[7] Elton, *The Practice of History*, pp. 10–11. Elton's definitions and view of methodology are of interest, since they do not arise out of, nor are they directed towards, biblical studies; rather, they are general in character.

[8] *Ibid.*, p. 12.

[9] C. F. D. Moule, *The Phenomenon of the New Testament* (London: SCM, 1967).

into existence of the Nazarenes', that is, an event, which called for an explanation. His own explanation is that the phenomenon was brought about by 'a most powerful and original mind and a tremendous confirmatory event'.[10] According to Moule, the existence of the Nazarenes is accounted for by the 'powerful and original mind' of Jesus and the event of his resurrection from the dead. I find this logic compelling. The phenomenon of the coming into existence of early Christianity is well attested. Its sudden emergence is as historically secure as any event in Palestine in that century. So the historian asks: what plausible explanation or explanations can be found for this event?

The social sciences and history

Not all, however, share the view of history given by Elton and illustrated by Moule. Those who apply social science to historical studies place their emphasis on what was, on the way things were, rather than on particular events and why they occurred. It is not too much to say that in the last quarter of the twentieth century this discipline and its ancillaries have revolutionized the study of history, including the study of antiquity and of Christian origins. A discipline that was once peripheral is now central, and one that was once central is now peripheral. Notable benefits for the understanding of the historical Jesus are claimed for the approach.[11] Social science figures prominently in current Jesus research.

Social science enquires into known groups of the time: for example, Pharisees, Sadducees and Essenes. An attempt is then made to understand Jesus in relation to such groups, whether belonging to the group, modifying it or opposing it. The methodology seeks to be 'holistic', that is, to paint a bigger canvas than the extant historical texts. Various background studies (such as Galilee studies) are also valued, even favoured, placing Jesus in a context in which to understand him. This approach asks, 'What were Jesus' *overall* aims?' and 'How does Jesus relate to Judaism or Galilee *globally*?'

But there are several problems with the method in regard to

[10] *Ibid.*, pp. 3, 17.

[11] T. Hatina, 'Jewish Religious Backgrounds of the New Testament', in *Approaches to New Testament Study*, ed. S. Porter (Sheffield: JSOT, 1995), pp. 48–49.

historical enquiry in general and into Christian origins in particular. First, dependence on social science rather than on the historical text tends to be speculative, with few controls. How can Jesus or any other historical figure from the period (for example, Herod the tetrarch or Pontius Pilate) be known apart from the texts which refer to him? Useful as background studies are in providing a social context for the person under review, they cannot portray the historical figure in the foreground. Only the specific texts, in this case the gospels, can do that.

Secondly, the method underestimates the influence of particular individuals upon the times in which they live. Social analysis can take us only so far in explaining the rise and impact of Herod the Great, for example. Certainly the emergence and influence of a Herod depended on the existence of propitious opportunities and circumstances; and in his case these did exist in the form of the weakness of the tail-end of the Hasmonean dynasts just as the Romans were encroaching into the eastern Mediterranean region. Yet the qualities which made Herod the Idumean 'great' ultimately elude analysis. How can social analysis explain *his* seizure of power? Josephus's portrayal of Herod as a prodigious athlete, fighter and leader[12] must be taken into account. Similar questions must be applied to Jesus. There were other prophets and rabbis in his general era. Why were they forgotten while he is remembered? The problem with the sociological approach is that it tends to limit great people to the social pool in which they are deemed to belong. It does not adequately account for the special qualities by which a very small number of people leave their imprint in history.

A third and more particular difficulty is that of data and distance. The social sciences depend on elaborate statistical data relating to such matters as income, education, peer associates, location of domicile and family history. Little information of this kind is available from the times of Jesus, and in the absence of hard evidence confident analysis is not possible.

A fourth problem relates to source material for the major factions of Jesus' time: the Dead Sea Scrolls, the New Testament, Josephus, the Mishnah, the Talmudim and so on. Daunting obstacles face the scholar in each set of sources. For example, there is a twofold related difficulty with the use of the Jewish

---

[12] *War* i.429–430.

sources, the Mishnah, Targumim and Talmudim. Not only are these texts much later than the era of Jesus, but significant changes occurred within the Judaism of the intervening years. By the time this literature was formulated the wars with Rome (AD 66–70 and 132–135) had been fought and lost. The world of the Mishnah (written *c.* AD 200) is very different from Jesus' world almost two centuries earlier. When the Mishnah was written, the high priests, the Sadducees, the Essenes and the Zealot-type revolutionaries no longer formed part of the landscape, as they had in Jesus' day. Moreover, gone were the various factions of the Pharisees, as they had existed up to AD 70; the movement was homogenized, and it was the era of Rabbinic Judaism. The Judaism of Herodian times, which had been inseparably Hebraic *and* Hellenistic, became now overwhelmingly Hebraic. To be sure, the later literature echoes the era of Jesus, with some traditions from Jesus' day surviving into the Mishnah, but it is a distant echo heard on the farther side of a wide cultural and historical chasm created by the wars throughout the period AD 66–135.

Certainly the texts of apocalyptic Judaism, the Qumran sectaries and Josephus, which are closer to Jesus, are valuable in recovering some aspects of the religious world of the first century. But there are problems of dating the apocalyptic texts and of establishing what connection Jesus himself may have had with these literatures. For example, the concept of the 'kingdom of God', which appears to have been so important in Jesus' teaching, is scarcely to be found in these terms in the texts of apocalyptic Judaism. In addition, some scholars no longer associate the Qumran texts exclusively with the Qumran community. Indeed, not all scholars agree that the buildings at Qumran were a religious settlement;[13] some suggest that the complex had a quite different purpose. Lastly, although Josephus, the historian who wrote during the later decades of the apostolic age, is our most valuable source for the general history of the era, he portrays the Jewish religion of Palestine not in recognizably Jewish terms, but as various 'philosophies', a category accessible to his Graeco-Roman readership familiar

---

[13] A. D. Crown and L. Cansdale, 'Qumran: Was it an Essene Settlement?' *BAR* 20/5 (1994), pp. 25ff. argue that the Qumran settlement was a trading-post for that region.

with Platonists, Stoics, Epicureans and Cynics. Notwithstanding these limitations, Josephus's writings do provide extensive understanding of the political, social and religious world of Jesus.

These criticisms do not amount to a rejection of the value of sociological analysis. To the degree to which it rests on appropriate sources, it assists in reconstructing Jesus' landscape, which in turn enhances our appreciation of him.[14] But the reconstructed context in itself tells us little of particular individuals, whether Herod or Jesus. Great and significant figures leave their mark on account of their greatness and significance. And it is the marks of their greatness left in the sources which are to be the particular interest of historical enquiry.

Events and interpretation

Throughout his study *The Practice of History*, Elton interacts with and criticizes the argument of E. H. Carr that historical knowledge cannot be separated from the interests of those involved. Historians' use of sources of 'fact', and the way they process those 'facts', both depend on human perception. According to Carr, history is 'a continuous process of interaction between the historian and his facts, an unending dialogue between the present and the past'.[15] But Elton questions this. It should not be assumed, he says, that no connection exists between the initial event and the record of it. Information about events and persons should not automatically be thought of as the artificial or arbitrary creation of those who have left the records. Rather, Elton argues, to a significant degree, people and events which impact on the course of life create their own evidence. This holds true whether we think of Herod 'the Great', Jesus of Nazareth or the outbreak of the Jewish war in AD 66. This is not to deny that the interests, competence and integrity of the authors of the sources need to be assessed. It is a fundamental part of the task of historians to identify the biases in their sources and also to be conscious of their own interests and worldviews.

---

[14] See *e.g.* B. Malina, *The New Testament World: Insights from Cultural Anthropology* (Louisville: Westminister John Knox, 1993).

[15] *What is History?* (Harmondsworth: Penguin, 1961), p. 30.

The way an individual creates his or her own evidence is illustrated in the account of John the baptizer and Jesus. Why is it that Jesus, rather than John, is called 'Christ'? John's claims to the title were, it could be argued, equal to or greater than those of Jesus. While both men had disciples, John came first and it was he who did the baptizing. Josephus devotes more space to John than to Jesus; he summarizes John's teachings, but not those of Jesus. John's ministry, like that of Jesus, attracted a large following. Jesus' words that there was no-one greater than John probably reflected the popular opinion. It is no surprise to hear from Luke that 'all men questioned in their hearts concerning John, whether perhaps he were the Christ', or from John's gospel that the Jerusalem religious establishment sent to ask John if he were the Christ.[16] John the baptizer, beheaded by an evil apostate Jew, Herod the tetrarch, was accorded the status of a martyred prophet by the Jews; whereas Jesus, being crucified for treason by the Romans, would have been regarded by Jews as accursed, being hanged upon a tree.[17] Finally, both men left behind them communities which revered them.[18] Yet it is a matter of history that the deaths of these two notable leaders issued in the preaching of not two messiahs, but of only one, Jesus. There is no evidence of any proclamation of John as Messiah, but there is extensive evidence of the proclamation of Jesus the Messiah. This is the more striking in that John was believed by some to have been raised from the dead.[19]

How is this distinction in roles to be accounted for? The most plausible explanation is that both John and Jesus distinguished their roles. Whereas John anticipated a successor, Jesus did not. Both John and Jesus saw John as forerunner and Jesus as 'he who [was] to come'.[20] In other words, the early apostles proclaimed Jesus as the Christ because that was Jesus' own view of himself. The resurrection alone cannot explain this proclamation of Jesus as Messiah since, as noted above, some also believed that John had been resurrected. While the resurrection of Jesus may have clinched the matter, it can have done so only

[16] Lk. 3:15; Jn. 1:19–20.

[17] Dt. 21:23; Acts 5:30; 10:39; 13:29; Gal. 3:13; 1 Pet. 2:24.

[18] In the case of John see Acts 18:24 – 19:7. P. Winter, 'The Proto-Source of Luke 1', *NovT* 1 (1956), pp. 184–200, argued that much of Luke 1 was originally a baptist document.

[19] Mk. 6:14.   [20] Mt. 11:3, 10.

on the basis that Jesus himself first believed himself to have been the Messiah and that he had established his messianic identity firmly in the minds of the disciples beforehand. In short, Jesus' own view of himself in turn became the apostles' view, and it is this view which permeates the New Testament.

All sources must be surveyed

Historical enquiry – the investigation of phenomena and their explanation – is dependent upon sources of information. According to Elton, 'Ideally the student should never consider less than the total of the historical material which may conceivably be relevant.'[21] This is difficult for the study of history for which there are masses of source materials. But this generally is not the case in the era of Jesus. All sources can be marshalled and considered, and there is no excuse for failure to do so. Elton helpfully comments that 'Historical research does not consist, as beginners in particular often suppose, in the pursuit of some particular evidence which will answer a particular question; it consists of an exhaustive, and exhausting, review of everything that may conceivably be germane to a given investigation.' Properly observed, he continues, this principle provides a safeguard against the dangers of prejudiced selection of evidence.[22] Broad-based interpretation of all relevant information conducted in the awareness of one's own personal 'blinkers' is fundamental to historical enquiry.

This procedure, however, has not always been followed. Jesus studies have tended to limit their enquiry to the gospels set against a preferred context, but without regard to the Acts of the Apostles or the New Testament letters. Moreover, not all the gospel evidence is used. Scholars have tended to choose a class of texts relating, for example, to Jesus as miracle-worker or to Jesus as teacher, or even a subset of those texts, leaving the remainder out of reckoning. The exclusive use which has been made of the hypothetical Q source,[23] with little reference to other gospel strands, is a further example. Based on selective

[21] Elton, *The Practice of History*, p. 66.   [22] *Ibid.*, pp. 66–67.

[23] 'Q' derives from the German *Quelle*, 'a source', and is a term applied to a source believed to be common to Matthew and Luke and which, as reconstructed, mainly consists of sayings of Jesus. For a review of various opinions on the existence of Q and its roles, see G. N. Stanton, *Gospel Truth* (London: HarperCollins, 1995), pp. 63–76. Stanton, who argues that the

choice of texts, a narrow role for Jesus is determined, whether 'Cynic', 'sage,' 'subversive sage', 'humane apocalyptist', or 'reasonable visionary'. A high degree of subjectivity is implied by a concentration on some texts and the relegation of others. Bultmann's dictum about the difficulty of presupposition-less exegesis remains true.

Thorough scholarship, it should be emphasized, addresses all the sources.

Incidental sources deserve careful notice

The neglect of the New Testament letters by current scholarship represents a particular failure in historical method. According to Elton, a distinction must be made between evidence produced specifically for the historian's attention, and that produced for another purpose.[24] The gospels and Acts would fit into Elton's first category, comprising, 'in the main, evidence of a literary and often secondary kind: chronicles, memoirs, notes of self-justification, letters intended for publication'. The letters of the New Testament, however, belong to the second category, 'that produced for another purpose'; these are 'the products of the ordinary events of life'.[25] Whereas the gospels and Acts are, as it were, the official records about Jesus and the history of the church, the letters are incidental documents addressing current issues in the churches, 'the ordinary events of life'. Because they are innocent of any attempt to convey new information about the historical Jesus, such information as they do contain, being incidental, is the more valuable and must be taken carefully into account.

To our loss this information is for the most part ignored by the Jesus-studies movement. The major weakness of the method is its failure to consider Jesus in terms of his immediate impact, that is, in the existence of the early church, its momentum and trajectory. This is a failure to begin at the beginning, with the study of the earliest written documentary evidence for Jesus, that is with the letters of the New Testament, especially the

---

existence of Q is 'a valid working hypothesis' (p. 71), though not an oral but a documentary tradition (p. 68), questions the view that there were various layers, such as Q1, Q2 and Q3. Stanton's proposal (pp. 75–76) that Q can be thought of as a written gospel is unconvincing. See also, with bibliography, E. Linnemann, 'The Lost Gospel of Q – Fact or Fantasy?' *TJ* 17 (1996), pp. 3–18.

[24] Elton, *The Practice of History*, p. 77.   [25] *Ibid.*

letters of Paul. This present work seeks to redress the imbalance, in particular by examining the letters of the New Testament.

Distant sources are problematic

Historical enquiry begins by assembling all the sources. These will be classified according to proximity to the event, type of source (for example, a gospel or a letter), original intended readership, original intended purpose, perceived interest or bias, intellectual competence, and so on. It is a basic, common-sense task which, above all, must be conducted in a right spirit in relationship to the sources. Sources which are distant from the event and which cannot be shown to rest on data closer to it are to be treated with appropriate critical caution.

In this regard, the use of the non-canonical or apocryphal gospels, in particular the *Gospel of Thomas* (for instance, by Koester and Crossan) is problematic. Historical method requires that all the sources be considered, with due weight given to early and underived sources. The *Gospel of Thomas* was written in the second century in Egypt, in a non-Palestinian religious ethos which is overtly gnostic. Whatever traces of Jesus' words and actions may be recovered in the *Gospel of Thomas*, this work is removed from the world of Jesus by a considerable passage of time and by the religious culture of a different country. The *Muratorian Canon* and the *Anti-Marcionite Prologues*, which belong to the second century,[26] speak of a fourfold gospel canon, and specifically exclude other gospels from the church's canon. Tatian (*c.* AD 170) combined the four gospels into one corpus. Its title, *Diatessaron*[27] ('through four'), significantly points to the early fixity of *four* gospels. The early recognition of four gospels is historically secure. Yet Koester and Crossan depend on later and rejected works like the *Gospel of Thomas* while making minimal use of the canonical gospels. J. P. Meier, who acknowledges the worth of having a greater pool of information about Jesus than we have in the canonical gospels, nevertheless comments that 'to call upon the Gospel of Peter or

---

[26] For a defence of the second-century dating of the Muratorian Fragment see L. Ferguson, 'Canon Muratori: Date and Provenance', *SP* XVII.2 (1982), pp. 677–683; L. M. McDonald, 'The Integrity of the Biblical Canon in Light of its Historical Development', *BBR* 6 (1996), pp. 95–132.

[27] Eusebius, *Historia Ecclesiastica* IV.29.6–7.

the Gospel of Thomas is to broaden out our pool of sources from the difficult to the incredible'.[28]

A number of scholars make use of the *Gospel of Thomas* together with the hypothetical Q document as a means of attacking the traditional and orthodox view of Jesus as set out in the canonical gospels and the remainder of the New Testament.[29] *Thomas* reproduces sayings of Jesus, but has little interest in his death and resurrection. Likewise Q concentrates on the sayings and lacks concern for the life, death and resurrection of Jesus. But both sources are problematic. As noted above, *Thomas* is late, remote and derived. Q is quite hypothetical, being without external reference by Paul, the early fathers, or the early manuscripts. Neither *Thomas* nor Q *alone* poses a threat to the views of the canonical gospels or to apostolic belief. Nevertheless, when placed in an alliance, as by a number of scholars,[30] they can be marshalled to attack the presentation of Jesus as we find it in the New Testament. But two flawed hypotheses do not produce one flawless one.

Conclusion

I have offered a definition of history and accompanying canons of practice. This definition and these canons reveal significant weaknesses in the processes of historical enquiry adopted by some currently engaged in Jesus research. I have argued that the practice of history focuses on events and changes of states from one thing to another, and on what explanations there might be for these phenomena. Social analysis, the study of the things that are or were, is of qualified value in regard to the study of antiquity in general and of Jesus specifically. Frequently those engaged in such studies depend on socially related studies more than on the extant texts. Textual study, where it occurs, is often eclectic, concentrating now on Jesus as healer, now on him as

[28] J. P. Meier, *A Marginal Jew: Rethinking the Historical Jesus* 1 (New York: Doubleday, 1991), pp. 140–141.

[29] For a rebuttal of these views, see W. R. Farmer, *The Gospel of Jesus: The Pastoral Relevance of the Synoptic Problem* (Louisville: Westminister John Knox, 1994), pp. 3–4; E. Linnemann, 'The Lost Gospel of Q – Fact or Fantasy?', *TJ* 17 (1996), pp. 3–18.

[30] See *e.g.* S. Patterson, 'Q the Lost Gospel', *BR* IX/5 (October 1993), pp. 35ff.

prophet, sage or reformer. There is a tendency to ignore some of the evidence and to place insufficient weight on evidence closest to Jesus, in particular the letters of Paul. These letters, along with others, deserve special attention since they were not written with the intention of providing historical information about Jesus, but dealt with 'the ordinary events of life'. They none the less bore incidental and implicit witness to the impact of a powerful figure in their recent past. The failure of scholars to include these epistolary data and to give due weight to them is perhaps the most signal failure of all.

Chapter Two

Christ in history

The scholars of current Jesus research, like their counterparts in the late nineteenth century, are preoccupied with the historical Jesus, as they seek to reconstruct him. The figure who is emphasized by both Christian and non-Christian sources in the aftermath of his historical span, to put it broadly but accurately, is not 'Jesus' but 'Christ'. As I shall propose, there is a historical connection between the Christians and Christ; they were given their name on account of his name and their devotion to the one who had that name. The Christians were devoted to Christ, confessed him, worshipped him, proclaimed him and took their impetus from him. But this Christ-impetus, this connectedness between Christ and the early Christians, so often observed then by non-Christian and Christian alike, is absent from many enquiries into the historical Jesus today. Thus an important element in getting back from the Christ of early Christianity to the historical Jesus, namely his impact or 'knock-on effect', tends to be ignored.

Christ through Christian eyes: *Christianoi*, Messiah-people

A new religious movement, Christianity, arose in the eastern Mediterranean during the principate of the Roman emperor Tiberius (AD 14–37). Although having small beginnings in Judea, it soon broke out of that province and within the next decade had come to the attention of the people of Antioch, the great metropolis of Syria. Its adherents had been both noticed and named: *Christianoi*, 'Messiah's people'.[1] Their leaders were

[1] Acts 11:26. *Christianoi* has a Latin ending, *-ianus*, meaning 'adherents of *Christ*/Messiah'. The name was probably coined by Romans, quite possibly

29

proclaimers, whose message was about one Jesus, the Christ or Messiah of the Jews. Clearly, it was this Christ who gave impulse to their message and their movement.

The movement spread rapidly to other places, including Rome, the centre of the empire. In his letter to the Romans, written in the mid-50s, Paul claims to have proclaimed the gospel in an arc from Jerusalem to Illyricum (the former Yugoslavia).[2] By that time (that is, within twenty years of Jesus, to put it quite conservatively)[3] the movement had also reached the Eternal City; the letter is addressed to believers in Rome. The same picture emerges from the Acts of the Apostles. Acts 13 – 18 narrates the missionary journeys of Paul in the late 40s and early 50s from Antioch to the interior of Asia Minor and on to the provinces of Asia, Macedonia and Achaia. According to Acts there were believers in Rome when Paul arrived there in the early 60s.[4] The rapid westwards spread of the movement and its early arrival in Rome must be regarded as historically secure.

An account of the origin and growth of the movement narrated from within was provided by the two-volume work, Luke-Acts. But like the Roman sources to be considered next, Luke-Acts sees Jesus Christ as providing the impetus for the movement. If Luke's first volume narrated what Jesus *began* to do and to teach in Galilee and Judea, the second narrates what he *continued* to do and teach, through the Holy Spirit working in his apostles from Jerusalem to the 'ends of the earth', Rome.[5]

Christians through non-Christian eyes

In time, the Christians would also leave their mark in non-Christian historical sources. The non-Christian perceptions of the Christians and their movement are full of historical interest.

---

signalling initial political disquiet about a movement associated with a messianic figure. In time the word was applied to the members of this movement, without special messianic connotations, as *e.g.* in a graffito in Pompeii of AD 62–79, and in Tacitus, Pliny and Suetonius. A parallel is seen in the word *Augustiani*, a name given to the supporters of the Emperor Nero. See further C. K. Barrett, *The Acts of the Apostles* 1 (Edinburgh: T. and T. Clark, 1994), pp. 556–557, with references.

[2] Rom. 15:19.

[3] See Rom. 15:23 ('I have longed for *many* years to come to you').

[4] Acts 28:15.

[5] Acts 1:8. *Psalms of Solomon* 8:16 points to Rome as 'the end of the earth'.

These writers tend to notice arresting characteristics of the new religion not always observed by modern historians.[6]

Chronologically, the first recorded incident involving Christians found in a non-Christian writer is Claudius's expulsion of Jews from Rome in AD 49. The writer, Suetonius,[7] notes that Claudius expelled the Jews from the city because of 'disturbances impulsore Chresto, at the instigation of Chrestus'.[8] This brief detail, though disputed as to both meaning and significance, is probably a reference to the Christian Jews. destabilizing the Jewish community of Rome by their proclamation of Jesus Christus.[9] We infer that Christ was the 'impulse', first for the proclamation, and then, as a consequence, for the civil disturbances which led the emperor indiscriminately to expel all the Jews, Christian and non-Christian, from Rome.[10]

The next reference to the movement was in relation to the fire which destroyed the greater part of the city in AD 64. Our chief source of information is the great Roman historian, Tacitus. Though a boy of seven at the time, Tacitus will not have failed to hear of the great fire and its aftermath.[11] He will have remembered that Nero's wrath was directed to the Christians as suitable scapegoats for starting the fire. In any case, as one who would later become a consul of Rome, Tacitus

[6] See e.g. R. Wilken, Christians as the Romans Saw Them (New Haven: Yale University Press, 1984), pp. 1 67.

[7] Suetonius, who had been secretary to the emperor Hadrian and who had access to state documents, wrote his Lives of the Caesars c. AD 120.

[8] Suetonius, Claudius xxv.4. The spelling of e for i was fairly widespread and is not thought to be a decisive argument against Chrestus = Christus (cf. Tertullian, Apology 3). See generally F. F. Bruce, 'Christianity under Claudius', BJRL 44 (1962), pp. 315–318. E. A. Judge and G. S. R. Thomas, 'The Origin of the Church at Rome', RTR xxv (1966), pp. 81–92 suggest that Chrestus was not Jesus the Messiah, but a messianic pretender whose name has not survived. To be questioned are the arguments of J. Murphy-O'Connor, St Paul's Corinth (Wilmington: Glazier, 1983), pp. 130–140, that Orosius's dating of Suetonius, Claudius xxv.4 to Claudius's ninth year (i.e. AD 49–50) is unfounded, and that the Suetonius incident is the same as that described in Dio Cassius 60:6.6, which occurred in AD 41. D. Slingerland, 'Suetonius Claudius 25.4 and the Account in Dio Cassius', JQR 79 (1989), pp. 305–322, has convincingly shown that Dio and Suetonius are referring to different events.

[9] So F. F. Bruce, New Testament History (London: Oliphants, 1969), p. 281.

[10] Cf. Acts 18:1–2.

[11] The details of Tacitus's birthplace, upbringing and early life are uncertain.

was well placed to know the official account of the fire and of the onslaught against this 'superstition'. (A *superstitio* was a sect based on fanatical beliefs, not recognized by, and therefore contrary to, the Roman state.)[12]

Years later, as governor of the province of Asia, he would write in his *Annals of Imperial Rome*[13] an account of both the fire and the action that was taken against the Christians.[14] Having mentioned the Christians, whom Tacitus spurns for their 'hatred of the human race' (that is, for their aloofness from Roman society), he takes a moment to give an account of the origin of the movement and its subsequent history. The 'Christians' took their name from a certain 'Christ', who had been executed (for treason, one supposes) in Judea by the governor Pontius Pilate. This had been during Tiberius' reign. But the movement, temporarily checked, immediately 'broke out afresh', not only in Judea where it began, but also in Rome, where by the time of the great fire it had become multitudinous, and, we infer, a matter of political concern.

Suetonius also mentions the punishment of Christians during the principate of Nero, though he does not connect it, as Tacitus does, to the fire of Rome in AD 64: 'Punishment was also inflicted on the Christians, a class of men given to a new and wicked superstition.'[15] Suetonius' statement is written in the context of the time he wrote, in the next century, rather than at the time of the fire. By that time Christianity was a movement of some dimensions ('a class of men'), though now sufficiently well known to need little further comment from Suetonius.

The third mention of the movement comes from the Jewish historian, Josephus, writing from Rome *c.* AD 95.[16] His account, though primarily concerned with the execution of Jesus sixty years earlier, pointedly notes that the 'tribe of Christians . . . has still not disappeared'. Though this Jesus was merely a 'wise man'

---

[12] See generally Wilken, *Christians as the Romans Saw Them*, pp. 48–67, who quotes Cicero and Plutarch (pp. 60–61). According to Cicero, 'Religion has been distinguished from superstition not only by philosophers but by our ancestors. [Superstition implied] groundless fear of the gods' (*On the Nature of the Gods* 1.117; 2.72). Plutarch states that the superstitious man 'enjoys no world in common with the rest of mankind' (*On Superstition* 166c).

[13] Written between about AD 115 and 117.   [14] *Annals* xv.44.2–5.

[15] Suetonius, *Nero* xvi.2.   [16] *Antiquities* xviii.63–64.

(a rabbi) and a miracle-worker, it was claimed – either by him or by his followers, or both – that he was 'the Christ'.[17] For this he was executed by Pilate upon information from the Jewish leaders. Josephus appears mystified that the 'tribe of Christians' – signifying a group of some size – had not yet disappeared with the death of its founder, the '[so-called] Christ'.

The fourth notice comes from Pliny, governor of the province of Bithynia, c. AD 112. Pliny was a friend of Tacitus, governor of Asia, the adjoining province. Both men express abhorrence of the new movement. Pliny gives by far the longest account of the Christians, which is set out in a letter to the emperor Trajan, seeking advice as to the trial and punishment of Christians. Pliny, however, gives no details about Jesus or the origin of the movement, which, it is inferred, the emperor and his proconsul already knew. Pliny notes with concern that 'this contagious *superstitio*' had reached the province more than twenty years earlier and that it had destroyed local religious practices and touched every stratum and group of the community. Pliny's gravest concern, however, is that the adherents have a loyalty to Christ greater than to the emperor. They will die rather than curse Christ and worship the emperor and the gods. In their private gatherings they sing hymns to Christ as a god (or as God).[18] Pliny's observations are stunning. The Christians worship Christ alone as God. They will not curse him, and they will not worship the emperor of Rome or the gods of Rome.

The comments of the Roman writers Suetonius, Tacitus, Josephus[19] and Pliny, though brief, are significant. Each author speaks of 'Christians'. This name had its origin in Roman Antioch in the mid-40s, being applied to the disciples by the people of the city.[20] In another Roman city, Thessalonica, it was

[17] Josephus's words, 'He was the Christ', are almost certainly not original to him. In a later section of the *Antiquities* Josephus refers to Jesus as 'the supposed Christ' (xx.200). It is likely that these or similar words originally occurred in the *Testimonium Flavianum*. The words 'tribe of the Christians', which are not in dispute, appear to relate back to a claim that this Jesus was 'the Christ'. See the excursus on p. 35.

[18] Pliny, *Epistle* 10.96. Pliny's words *carmen Christo quasi deo* are taken by M. Hengel, *Studies in Early Christology* (Edinburgh: T. and T. Clark, 1995), p. 263, as 'predicates of God [which] were applied to Christ'.

[19] Though a Jew and an apologist for Judaism, Josephus was writing from Rome, under the patronage of the Roman imperial family, the Flavians.

[20] Acts 11:26.

complained that Paul and Silas were saying that there was 'another king, Jesus', alongside or taking priority over the Roman emperor.[21] Consistent with their commitment to a superior king, these Christians would not participate in the state religion, worshipping the emperor and the gods. Rather, they were members of a private sect, a *superstitio*. The people of the Graeco-Roman east were pleased to worship the Roman Caesar as a 'saviour' and 'benefactor'.[22] But not these Christians. In Roman eyes, they were guilty of 'hatred of the human race'.[23]

Through Roman eyes we observe a striking characteristic of the movement, which many modern historians do not notice. What struck the Romans was the intensity of the connection between the Christians and Christ. Roman loyalty to Caesar and the state was the fundamental expectation of all members of society, with the sole exception of the Jews. Romans, therefore, took powerful, even shocked, exception to the Christians' loyalty to this 'other king'. Their commitment to Christ as king was unto death, and thus a loyalty greater than loyalty to the emperor. This loyalty, which was expressed in private gatherings of adherents, was seen as politically subversive. According to the Romans, as reported in the Acts and as stated in their own writings, a Christian was one who was devoted to Christ.

Conclusion

In terms of the logic of history there must have been some continuing impulse from the historical Jesus to the proclaimed Christ, some substantive continuity. But the Jesus of the manifold current reconstructions of Jesus research is in almost every case a future-less Jesus, a Jesus who is going nowhere, except to historical oblivion. Jesus must have been a different and a greater figure to have catapulted into motion the movement which impacted the world of its day in the way it did. The evidence for this impact is clearly seen in the New

[21] Acts 17:6.

[22] The Christians' loyalty to Christ is in contrast with the readiness with which the peoples of the East gladly ascribed honour and worship to Caesar. An inscription from Augustus's era refers to him as 'the good Augustus . . . benefactor and saviour of the whole world' (quoted in N. Lewis and M. Reinhold, *Roman Civilization* II, New York: Harper, 1966, p. 64 n. 191).

[23] Tacitus's verdict on the Christians in Rome in *Annals* xv.44.5.

Testament and confirmed in the non-Christian sources.

This evidence points to a movement which arose in Palestine in the 30s and which spread rapidly to other parts of the empire, including to Rome itself. Jesus studies have tended to ignore the movement, concentrating rather on Jesus in his milieu, whether that milieu be reconstructed as Jewish or as Hellenistic. But the resulting Jesuses tend to be pale, unremarkable figures, taking whatever colour and character can be found for them from the social background that has been re-created for them.

The early rise of Christianity as a movement close in time to Jesus is a fact of history. *Someone* gave impulse to the rise of that movement in the immediately preceding weeks and months. Only a quite remarkable figure could have provided that percussive impulse. Historical probability, what I am calling the 'logic of history', demands nothing less. In short, the logic of history, when applied to the study of Jesus, means that the existence, momentum and direction of the early church are most plausibly explained by a powerful teacher who had a close relationship beforehand with his immediate circle, an influence radically reinforced by the confirmatory event of his resurrection from the dead. For us today and for all who have lived beyond the lifespan of Jesus, he can only be the Christ of faith. Nevertheless, that those who lived after the first Easter were people of such faith is itself not a matter of faith but a historical fact. From the fact of the faith of the apostles and first Christians as found in the New Testament and as confirmed by non-Christian sources, we are faced with the question: what gave rise to that faith, a faith which emerged in the immediate aftermath of Jesus, back to back with him, as it were? We stand on sure grounds of sound historical method when we reply that the Christ of the early church's faith was, without discontinuity, the truly historical figure Jesus of Nazareth. The one proclaimed by the apostle Peter on the day of Pentecost was the same Jesus of Nazareth ('this Jesus') whom God has now made Lord and Christ.

Excursus
Jesus as 'Christ' in the Testimonium Flavianum

It is almost universally agreed that Josephus's account of Jesus in *Antiquities of the Jews* xviii.63ff. has been the subject of three

Christian interpolations,[24] as denoted by the words italicized:

> At that time there appeared Jesus, a wise man, *if indeed one ought to call him a man.* For he was a doer of amazing deeds, a teacher of those who accept the truth with pleasure. He won over many of the Jews and many of the Greeks. *He was the Christ.* And when Pilate condemned him to the cross, the leading men among us having accused him, those who loved him from the start did not cease to do so. *For he appeared to them the third day alive again, the prophets of God having spoken these and myriad of other marvels about him.* And the tribe of Christians, named after him, has to this day not died out.

It is accepted that the first and third items are interpolations. As an apologist for Judaism Josephus is not likely to have acknowledged Jesus' deity (as here implied) or his resurrection on the third day, according to the prophets (which resonates with the *credo* of 1 Corinthians 15:5). But what of the second item: *He was the Christ?* Certainly its omission would appear justified by Origen's well-known assertion that Josephus did not believe Jesus to be the Christ (*Contra Celsum* i.47; *Commentary on Matthew* 10:17). This view of Josephus's scepticism seems to be confirmed later in the *Antiquities* when Josephus refers to the death of James, 'brother of Jesus, *the so-called Christ*'.[25]

There is a problem, however, if the words 'He was the Christ' are omitted altogether. In the first place, Josephus's rather mystified tones, 'the tribe of Christians, *named* after him', do not make sense unless the word 'Christ' appeared earlier. Named after whom? Jesus? Why would 'Christians' be named after 'Jesus'? The word 'Christ', connected to Jesus, must have appeared in the original for the text to make sense. The text as emended to omit the word 'Christ' has been over-emended. Secondly, why would a miracle-working 'wise man' be subject to

---

[24] See *e.g.* J. P. Meier, *A Marginal Jew: Rethinking the Historical Jesus* 1 (New York: Doubleday, 1991), pp. 56–69; C. A. Evans, 'Jesus in Non-Christian Sources', in *Studying the Historical Jesus*, ed. B. Chilton and C. A. Evans (Leiden: Brill, 1994), pp. 466–468.

[25] *Tou legomenou Christou, Antiquities* xx.200; *cf.* Jerome, *De viris illustribus* xiii, 'believed to be the Messiah'.

Roman trial (that is, accusation and condemnation) followed by *Roman* execution by crucifixion? No capital crime against Roman rule is implicit in Jesus' miracle-working or teaching *per se*. But if Jesus claimed to be the Christ, or if others claimed it for him, then this would be a matter of treason and subject to Roman action. Here Josephus's undisputed text from later in the *Antiquities*, that Jesus was 'the so-called Christ', accords well with the gospels' account of the Roman trial and execution of Jesus as 'king of the Jews'. Thus the missing element in the text is resolved simply by the inclusion of the words 'the so-called Christ', as in Josephus's later reference.

This emendation would satisfy Origen's reference to Josephus's agnosticism about Jesus as the Christ. Moreover, these words, or similar, are needed in the text, which as it stands does not make complete sense. The effect of this emendation is that both Josephus and Tacitus, our earliest non-Christian sources for the origins of Christianity, link the word 'Christian' with the man 'Christ' as the founder of the movement. This, in turn, is quite consistent with the New Testament writer who observes, 'if you are reproached for the name of *Christ*, you are blessed . . . if one suffers as a *Christian*, let him not be ashamed, but under that name let him glorify God.'[26] A Christian was one who had life-and-death loyalty to Christ.

[26] 1 Pet. 4:14, 16.

Chapter Three

Jesus in proclamation and tradition

We turn now to reflect on the role of the New Testament letters in establishing the impact of Jesus upon early Christianity. In my view, the letters rather than the gospels are the appropriate entry-point into the New Testament for an understanding of the significance of Jesus as the impulse for the rise of the early church.

The historian's task

The historian's initial task in any enquiry is to assemble the documentary sources available, which will then be classified in terms of genre and relative proximity to the subject. As we have already seen, it will be important to survey all the sources.[1]

The New Testament provides our major sources for any enquiry into Jesus and early Christianity. This corpus consists of twenty-seven documents which were written within approximately sixty years of Jesus' death. Broadly speaking, there are two classes of literature: letters and biographies. There are twenty-two letters of various lengths and kinds (if we include the Apocalypse, which has some epistolary characteristics).[2] Paul's thirteen letters make him the major contributor of this genre. The four gospels are biographies of Jesus,[3] with Acts as a second volume to the third. This second volume tells the story of Christ's continuing words and works, exercised through various people, especially Paul. Luke's two-part work makes him the major biographer and historian within the New Testament corpus.

---

[1] See above, pp. 24–25. [2] See Rev. 1:4; 2:1, 8, 12, 18; 3:1, 7, 14.
[3] See below, pp. 154–157.

Problems with the gospels and Acts as a point of entry

It might be supposed that the gospels and Acts would be the obvious place to begin establishing a 'history' of Jesus and the apostolic age. But there are three difficulties in such an approach. One is that each of the gospels is a final product, the work of an author who has woven together various sources into a document which is primarily historical and biographical in character and intent. This intentionally historical character expresses the author's motivation, indeed, his bias. His bias may be congruous with reality, or it may not. It is not immediately apparent, either way, from the gospels. But the letters have no such motivation, being written to those who are already persuaded to be Christians. Yet, as we shall see, the letters supply incidental, gratuitously given information about Jesus, which the historian will find very interesting. Not least, such information can be used to gauge the integrity or otherwise of the more deliberately written gospels. Thus the letters are, historically speaking, a preferred point of entry into Jesus studies.

Secondly, the gospels pose complex and as yet unresolved literary problems. What sources underlie the gospels? Do the gospels depend on one another? What is their interrelationship? How can we account for their similarities and their differences? To begin our historical enquiry into Jesus in the gospels means running into one dense thicket after another. The letters, notwithstanding their incorporation of pre-formed traditions, are more straightforward documents. A prior consideration of the letters may serve to remove in advance some of the obstacles that tend to block the way in the historical and biographical works.

Thirdly, the gospels and Acts cannot be dated with certainty, except that they post-date Jesus and pre-date the apostolic fathers. All that can be said with any measure of agreement is that they arose some time between AD 33, when Jesus died,[4] and

---

[4] For the AD 33 dating of the crucifixion see H. Hoehner, *Chronological Aspects of the Life of Christ* (Grand Rapids: Zondervan, 1977), pp. 95–114; C. J. Humphreys and W. G. Waddington, 'Astronomy and the Date of the Crucifixion', in *Chronos, Kairos, Christos* (Winona Lake: Eisenbrauns, 1989), pp. 165–181.

AD 100, when the post-apostolic writings began to appear. To begin with the gospels would mean opening up numerous variables regarding the dating of these documents, delaying a beginning of enquiry proper. As we shall now see, however, Paul's letters are both datable and close in time to Jesus.

Paul's letters and historical enquiry into early Christianity

The letters of the New Testament, in particular the letters of Paul, are the preferred point of historical entry to enquiry into Jesus and the apostolic age for three reasons. First, Paul's letters are the earliest written sources of information about Christianity. His earliest letter was written from Corinth in about AD 50 to the church in Thessalonica.[5] Here we find the first historical documentation of Christianity.

To be sure, Christianity did not begin with Paul, but with Jesus, whose ministry we date to about AD 28–33.[6] Moreover, some seventeen years of Christian history passed before Paul's first letter appeared. Paul himself refers to churches which had come into existence in Judea and with which he had no direct connection.[7] Nevertheless, Paul played an active part in the history of Christianity throughout those years, first as persecutor,[8] then as apostle from the time the resurrected Jesus appeared to him;[9] that is, from about AD 34.[10] Less than three years later he returned from Damascus to Jerusalem to enquire of (*historēsai*)[11] Cephas, with whom he stayed for fifteen days and

---

[5] That is, unless Galatians was written beforehand, as many believe, and for some good reasons. There is more than one side to the debate on the dating of Galatians. For an argument in favour of a South Galatian provenance, which is connected with the earlier dating, see F. F. Bruce, *Commentary on Galatians* (Exeter: Paternoster, 1982), pp. 5–18.

[6] See below, pp. 111–114.   [7] 1 Thes. 2:14; Gal. 1:22.

[8] Gal. 1:13, 21; Phil. 3:6.   [9] 1 Cor. 15:8.

[10] See H. N. Ridderbos, *Paul and Jesus* (Nutley: Presbyterian and Reformed, 1977), pp. 63–79.

[11] *Historēsai* is a NT hapax. The basic meaning is 'enquire into, or about, or from'. See Herodotus ii.19; iii.77; Polybius iii.48.12; Plutarch, *Moralia* 516C; and J. D. G. Dunn, 'The Relationship Between Paul and Jerusalem According to Gal i and ii', in *Jesus, Paul and the Law: Studies in Mark and Galatians* (London: SPCK, 1990), pp. 108–126.

where he also saw James, the brother of Jesus.[12] Through these meetings with the leading disciple on the one hand, and the eldest of Jesus' siblings on the other, Paul had extensive opportunity to hear about the historical Jesus.

Since there is evidence that Paul met his death under Nero in the aftermath of the fire of Rome in AD 64,[13] it is possible to set his letters within a specific time-frame, that is, between *c.* AD 50 (with the dispatch of the first letter to the Thessalonians) and his death *c.* AD 65. Not only are we able to fix the period in which these letters were written, but it appears almost certain that his earliest letters, including those written to the Thessalonians and the Corinthians, are the first written documents referring to Christianity,[14] emerging only twenty or so years after the historical Jesus.

Secondly, the Pauline letters have early as well as broad manuscript attestation. The variations between the manuscripts of the letters of Paul are of limited and secondary theological importance. In matters relating to Christian origins the text of Paul's letters, as read in the standard Greek editions and as rendered in the major translations, is not in dispute.[15]

Thirdly, the letters are a literary vehicle used by Paul to address issues current at the time of writing in the life of a church or churches physically distant from him. They are living letters written in response to letters and reports from the churches, now explaining, now clarifying, now correcting, now defending and now attacking. Specifically, the letters are not evangelistic tracts, seeking to win adherents or establish churches. Nor are they consciously written histories, designed to catch the eye of other historians. Rather, they address already existing assemblies of confessing believers, among whom the primary work of evangelism had already been done.

Thus the Pauline letters are much less complex, from a historical and literary point of view, than the gospels and Acts. We know the identity of the writer and we know that he was addressing a specific group of people at a particular time and place, and (in a number of cases) in circumstances that we are

---

[12] Gal. 1:18–19. [13] Clement of Rome, *Letter to the Corinthians* V–VI.

[14] Regarding the letter to the Galatians, it is a matter of debate as to when, whence and to whom, precisely, Paul wrote.

[15] See J. C. Beker, 'Contingency and Coherence in the Letters of Paul', *USQR* XXXIII (1978), pp. 141–151.

more or less able to reconstruct. The reader of Acts may raise sceptical eyebrows at Luke's descriptions of Paul's miracles, discounting them, perhaps, as the author's embellishment to give legitimacy to Paul. But where Paul himself reminds the Corinthians of 'signs, wonders and miracles done among' them, he is appealing to events which are eminently open to rebuttal. Had he not in fact performed miracles in Corinth, he would have invited even more scorn from the Corinthians.[16] Particularly important for the historian are Paul's gratuitous reminiscences about how the churches in Thessalonica and Corinth were founded, and the clear picture of the role of proclamation by Paul and others in that process.[17]

So, then, the datability, the closeness in time to Jesus and the beginnings of Christianity with which Paul was involved almost from the outset, together with the integrity of the extant text of the corpus and the contemporary issue-centred, incidental character of these letters, combine to make them the most appropriate place to begin enquiry into the nature and history of early Christianity.

Proclamation and tradition: the foundation of the churches in Thessalonica and Corinth

We learn from one of Paul's earliest letters that he came to Thessalonica, a major city in Macedonia, and proclaimed the gospel. In response a group of hearers committed themselves to Jesus Christ, and so the church in Thessalonica was born.[18] From the Corinthian letters we learn that his proclamation in Corinth was the means of the creation of the church there.[19] Clearly, the impulse for church formation was proclamation. But what did Paul proclaim? He proclaimed Jesus Christ.[20] The

[16] 2 Cor. 12:12.

[17] 1 Thes. 1:5, 2:16; 1 Cor. 2:1–5; 15:1–11; 2 Cor. 1:19; 12:12.

[18] 1 Thes. 1:5–8.   [19] 1 Cor. 2:1–5; 15:1–2; 2 Cor. 1:19; cf. 11:4.

[20] 2 Cor. 4:5; 11:4. This puts it rather baldly. M. Hengel, 'Origins', in his *Between Jesus and Paul* (London: SCM, 1983), is correct in saying, 'In antiquity it was quite impossible to proclaim as Kyrios, Son of God and Redeemer a man who had been crucified a few years earlier – i.e., an alleged criminal – without saying something about who this man was, what he taught and did and how and why he died' (p. 178, n. 73).

churches were assemblies of people who confessed and believed in Jesus.

From the first letters to these churches it emerges that, broadly speaking, a connected twofold process was involved in their foundation. On one hand there was the *proclamation* of the message of the gospel of Christ. On the other, when the hearers responded – whether as individuals or as a group – the apostle 'handed over' to them the *tradition*.

In the main Paul refers to proclamation by means of two verbs ('evangelize' and 'proclaim'), and these are, to a degree, interchangeable.[21] His tradition terminology, however, belongs consistently to the standard Jewish rabbinic vocabulary, as in, for example, 'I handed over' and 'you received'.[22] By these technical terms, Paul recollects the circumstances of the initial proclamation of the gospel and the formation of the church in Corinth. This vocabulary is particularly evident in Paul's earliest letters, 1 and 2 Thessalonians[23] and 1 Corinthians.[24]

'Proclaiming', by contrast, was part of Graeco-Roman culture.[25] In declaring that he was 'proclaiming' or 'evangelizing', Paul was placing himself alongside those officials who brought important public announcements to cities and towns from kings and emperors. There is a close connection in Paul's usage between proclaiming and 'traditioning'. Notice Paul's words in 1 Corinthians 15:1–3: 'I would remind you . . . in what terms I evangelized you the gospel . . . For I handed over (traditioned) to you what I also received' (my translation). Thus 'to evangelize' meant something like 'to hand over'[26] a body of information, that

---

[21] The fluidity of use between *euangelizomai/euangelion* and *kēryssō/kērygma* may be noted at 1 Cor. 1:17, 23; 2:4; 15:1–2, 11, 14. Paul can write, 'the gospel which I proclaim' (*to euangelion ho kēryssō*, Gal. 2:2, my translation).

[22] See *e.g.* Mk. 7:3–5, 8–9, 13; Gal. 1:14. *TDNT*, entries for *paradidōmi* and *paralambanō*.

[23] While it is held by many that 2 Thessalonians is not a primary Pauline work, the view taken here is that it is. See D. G. Guthrie, *New Testament Introduction* (Leicester: Apollos, 4th edn. 1990), pp. 592–599.

[24] 1 Thes. 2:13; 4:1–2; 2 Thes. 3:6; 1 Cor. 11:2, 23; 15:1, 2, 3. See B. Gerhardsson, *Memory and Manuscript* (Uppsala: Lund, 1964), pp. 288ff.

[25] This is true whichever vocabulary Paul is using, whether *kēryssein* or *euangelisesthai*. See respective entries in *TDNT*.

[26] Literally 'the gospel I evangelized you . . . *for* I handed over to you'.

is, 'what'[27] the hearers 'received'.[28] Paul proceeds to elaborate the 'what-ness'[29] of the gospel message in four statements, each beginning with 'that':

that Christ – the Messiah, the Son of David – died for our sins
that he was buried
that he was raised the third day . . .
that he appeared . . .

Paul sums up this message in a variety of ways in 1 Corinthians, in the phrases 'evangelize . . . the cross', 'the word of the cross', 'proclaim Christ [= the Messiah] crucified', 'Jesus Christ and him crucified', and 'proclaiming . . . the scandal of the cross'.[30] Paul, however, does not restrict this primary message to Christ crucified and risen. He also refers to the proclamation of the 'Son of God, Jesus Christ',[31] or simply to proclaiming 'Jesus Christ as Lord'.[32]

In letters to other churches Paul also uses the technical language of rabbinic 'traditioning' – the handing over not of an impersonal body of information, however, but of a person, 'Christ'. In evocatively rabbinic language he admonishes the Colossians: 'As therefore you *received* Christ Jesus the Lord, so *walk* in him . . . established in the faith, just as you were taught . . . [not] according to the *tradition* of men . . . [but according to] Christ.'[33] Here is a 'tradition' which these Lycus Valley believers 'received' from Epaphras, which went back to Christ, mediated to Epaphras by Paul, a *halakhah* (a Christian 'walking'), which they had been 'taught'. But it is 'Christ Jesus the Lord' whom they have 'received' in that body of teaching. The same rabbinic vocabulary, also personalized to Christ, is

---

[27] *Cf.* 1 Cor. 15:1–3, *to euangelion ho . . . ho kai . . . en hō kai . . . di' hou . . .* See, too, Gal. 1:9, 12.

[28] For references to the gospel as something 'received', see 1 Cor. 15:2; 2 Cor. 11:4; *cf.* Gal. 1:9.

[29] The objectivity of the message is conveyed by his words (literally), 'He evangelizes the faith' (*euangelizetai tēn pistin*, Gal. 1:23; *cf.* 2 Cor. 13:5).

[30] 1 Cor. 1:17, 18, 23; 2:2; Gal. 5:11 (my translations).

[31] 2 Cor. 1:18–19; *cf.* 1 Thes. 1:10.   [32] 2 Cor. 4:4.

[33] Col. 2:6–8, my translation. While many take Colossians to be deutero-Pauline, this is not the view taken here. Few dispute the Pauline authorship of Philemon. Yet Philemon and Colossians are connected historically. See Phm. 1, 23 and Col. 1:7; 4:10, 14–17.

used in the letter to the Ephesians. He reminds the readers, 'you did not so *learn Christ* – assuming you have heard *him* and been taught in *him*, as the truth is in *Jesus*.'[34] But this refers to their evangelization, as recollected earlier in the letter: 'you heard the word of truth, the gospel of your salvation, and have believed in him [Christ]'.[35] In consequence, the lifestyle of these believers is described as a 'walk', a *halakhah*. He exhorts, 'walk in love . . . walk as children of light . . . look carefully . . . how you walk'.[36]

This is consistent with reminiscences of his gospel ministry in Thessalonica and Corinth. From these, we conclude that what Paul proclaimed and traditioned about Jesus was that Jesus was the Christ/Messiah, the Son of God, who was crucified for sins, buried, raised the third day, and seen alive on many occasions subsequently, who is now Lord, and who will return.[37]

Paul's 'traditioning' was by no means exhausted, however, by these references to Jesus' death, resurrection and return. The tradition of the Lord's Supper which he had 'received' he also handed on ('delivered') to the Corinthians: that is, what Jesus did and said 'on the night when he was betrayed'.[38] It is evident, too, that Paul 'handed over' to the churches various of the 'commands' and 'traditions' of Jesus which Paul himself had received: for example, in regard to marriage, the payment of ministers and the suddenness of the Lord's return.[39] Two great teachings of Jesus, that God is *Abba*, 'Father', and that the persecuted were to bless their persecutors, were known to Paul and handed on by him to the churches.[40] Some churches are commended for holding to the traditions which Paul had handed over to them[41] while others are exhorted to stand fast in such traditions.[42] Paul's words, 'So then, brethren, stand firm

---

[34] Eph. 4:20–21, my translation.   [35] Eph. 1:13.   [36] Eph. 5:1, 8, 15; *cf.* 2.10.
[37] So 1 Thes. 1:10; 5:2; 1 Cor. 1:7; 15:3–8.
[38] 1 Cor. 11:23–25. The words 'on the night when he was betrayed' signal a larger narrative tradition, perhaps even a version of the passion narrative, from which he now selects a part.
[39] 1 Cor. 7:10 (*cf.* 1 Thes. 4:2); 9:14; 1 Thes. 4:15; 5:2. Paul's relatively infrequent quotation of Jesus may be due to his awareness of the Jerusalem apostles' first-hand knowledge of this teaching; over-use might expose Paul to contradiction and call into question his authority. See A. J. M. Wedderburn, 'Paul and Jesus', *SJT* 38 (1985), p. 191.
[40] Rom. 8:15; Gal. 4:6 (*cf.* Mk. 14:36); Rom. 12:14; 1 Cor. 4:12 (Mt. 5:44). See further J. Jeremias, 'The Key to Pauline Theology', *ExpT* 76 (1964–5), p. 30.
[41] Rom. 6:17; 1 Cor. 11:2.   [42] Phil. 4:9; 2 Thes. 2:15; 3:6.

and hold to the traditions which you were taught by us, either by word of mouth or by letter',[43] well summarize Paul's ministry to these churches. Paul can even assume that a church he had not visited had had 'handed over' (*paradothēte*) to it a 'pattern (*typos*) of teaching'.[44] In Romans 12 – 15 Paul makes frequent allusions to a Jesus-tradition in such a way as to suggest that he thought his readers would be aware of it.[45]

The greater part of his letters, addressed as they are to issues then current, are by way of reminder or application in regard to the 'traditions' he passed on to the churches when he evangelized them.[46] But it is clear from his reminiscences made in passing that Paul's proclamation of Jesus Christ was the impulse that founded the churches which he established.

Christ in 2 Corinthians

The technical rabbinic language for 'handing over' and 'receiving' the tradition, so powerful in 1 Corinthians, does not occur in 2 Corinthians. Nevertheless, we have echoes in the later letter of Paul's initial gospel penetration in Corinth six years earlier. According to these, Paul proclaimed Jesus in at least three ways: as Son of God, the Christ/Messiah and Lord.[47] It is the more striking, therefore, given the absence of the 'tradition' vocabulary, and in the light of these exalted Christological titles, that Paul refers in the way he does to biographical details about Jesus.[48] Consider the following

---

[43] 2 Thes. 2:15.   [44] Rom. 6:17.

[45] See generally in regard to Romans M. Thompson, *Clothed with Christ: The Example and Teaching of Jesus in Rom 12.1 – 15.13*, *JSNT* Supplement Series 59 (Sheffield: JSOT, 1991). *Cf.* D. C. Allison, 'The Pauline Epistles and the Synoptic Gospels: The Patterns of the Parallels', *NTS* 28 (1982), pp. 1–32; S. Kim, 'Jesus, Sayings of', in *DPL*, pp. 474–492; G. N. Stanton, *Jesus of Nazareth in New Testament Preaching*, *SNTS* Monograph Series 27 (Cambridge: Cambridge University Press, 1974).

[46] Whether traditions he had himself received or those which he had formulated (2 Thes. 3:6, 10).

[47] 2 Cor. 1:19; 2:12 (*cf.* 4:4; 9:13; 10:14); 4:5. For discussion see L. Belleville, 'Gospel and Kerygma', in *Gospel and Paul*, ed. L. A. Jervis and P. Richardson (Sheffield: JSOT, 1994), pp. 137–140.

[48] See R. V. G. Tasker, 'St Paul and the Earthly Life of Jesus', *ExpT* 46 (1934–5), pp. 557–562, who sees a 'Lukan feeling and character' reflected in 2 Corinthians. Tasker comments that 'it is then certainly not true that the Jesus of history plays little or no part in the essential Christian thought of St Paul' (p.

phrases:[49] 'The Son of God, Jesus Christ' (1:19); 'your slaves for *Jesus'* sake' (RSV mg.), or 'your slaves because Jesus was' (my translation) (4:5);[50] 'the dying of *Jesus*' (4:10, my translation);[51] 'handed over to death for *Jesus'* sake', or 'handed over to death, because Jesus was' (4:11, my translations);[52] 'knowing that he who raised the Lord *Jesus* . . .' (4:14); '*one* has died for all' (5:14); '*him* who knew no sin God made to be sin' (5:21, my translation); 'though . . . rich . . . *he* became poor' (8:9); 'the meekness and gentleness of *Christ*' (10:1); and '[*Christ*] was crucified in weakness' (13:4).

The above lead us to the following observations.

First, there is a biographical-theological sweep of Jesus' life. Paul refers to an incarnation from wealth to a lifestyle of poverty. He speaks of a sinless man, the Son of God, Jesus Christ, who exercised a ministry which was meek and gentle. He was a slave for others by dying, culminating in his identification with sinners in his substitutionary death by crucifixion for them. This was followed by his resurrection for them from the dead.

Mere reference to the crucifixion of Jesus would prompt many questions from hearers, whether Jews or Gentiles, which would have led the apostle to give further details about Jesus of Nazareth. The Corinthians would ask, 'Who was he?' 'Where did he come from?' 'What was he like?' At that time the crucifixion was not so much a visible or theological symbol (as it would become), but an event involving a person in the recent past,

---

562). D. Wenham, 'The Story of Jesus Known to Paul', in *Jesus of Nazareth: Lord and Christ*, ed. J. B. Green and M. Turner (Grand Rapids: Eerdmans, 1994), pp. 297–311, finds in Paul's writings allusions to the birth of Jesus, his baptism and temptations, the mission and miracles of the twelve during Jesus' ministry, and the transfiguration. Wenham points out that Paul's relative silence about Jesus ought not to imply ignorance. Paul reminds the Corinthians about the Lord's Supper and Jesus' resurrection appearances only because of acute problems on these issues in Corinth at the time. J. D. G. Dunn, 'Jesus Tradition in Paul', in *Studying the Historical Jesus*, ed. B. Chilton and C. Evans (Leiden: Brill, 1994), pp. 155–178, also reaches an affirmative conclusion as to the considerable extent of knowledge of Jesus' words and deeds shared by Paul and his congregations.

[49] For discussion see Belleville, 'Gospel and Kerygma', pp. 140–156.

[50] *Doulous hymōn dia Iēsoun. Dia* + the accusative is here taken in the sense 'on account of Jesus', that is, implying that Jesus is the model or example.

[51] *Tēn nekrōsin tou Iēsou*, referring to the process of 'dying', *i.e.*, to the totality of Jesus' ministry.

[52] *Eis thanaton paradidometha dia Iēsoun.*

provoking many questions about that person. Proclamation about the crucifixion of Jesus would have stimulated many questions about him and secured appropriate answers. As a consequence, members of the churches must have had a reasonable understanding about the historical Jesus.

Secondly, Paul's choice of allusions is nevertheless limited to elements which point consistently to Christ's humility, service for others and generosity, but, above all, to his sufferings, death and resurrection. By no means does it provide a complete picture of Jesus. Such references are chosen by Paul because they reinforce his message to the Corinthians of the non-triumphalist, serving nature of apostleship and of the Christian life, exercised in the reality of weakness. The historical context of the letter determines, to a degree, the historical detail about Jesus to which Paul will appeal. Near the beginning of the letter Paul refers to 'Christ's sufferings'[53] a term also used in 1 Peter 4:13, signifying, perhaps, a traditional body of information on which both apostles depended.

Thirdly, Paul mentions such characteristics of Jesus without further ado; both he and his readers know the point he is making. Evidently he is appealing to what they know about Jesus; that is, what they had come to know about Jesus from Paul when he established the church in Corinth.[54] Presumably, Paul could make other allusions to Jesus, if the need arose, and the Corinthians would understand what he meant.

A survey of the Thessalonian and Corinthian correspondence, then, is sufficient to draw attention to the fact that proclamation about Jesus was tied to historical information about him. More complete information about Jesus in Paul's letters would emerge from a thorough investigation of the corpus (see the excursus at the end of this chapter).[55]

[53] 2 Cor. 1:5.

[54] So J. D. G. Dunn, *Unity and Diversity in the New Testament* (London: SCM, 1977), p. 68.

[55] *Cf.* A. J. M. Wedderburn, 'Paul and the Story of Jesus', in *Paul and Jesus* (Sheffield: JSOT, 1989), pp. 161–189, who sees the 'story' of Jesus (which he does not regard as 'myth') as being made to fulfil what was needed, rather than what was necessarily historically true.

Jesus in Paul: summary and conclusion

Three straightforward observations should be made. One is that the churches in Thessalonica and Corinth came into existence as a result of Paul's proclamation to them about Jesus Christ. The second is that this proclaimed figure was exalted; he is the Christ, the Son of God the Lord. Yet, thirdly, this person, Jesus, was one about whom biographical information was known, probably though the process of the initial preaching and 'handing over' of various 'received traditions' to the churches, and from their questions and his answers. Jesus Christ as proclaimed – the impulse for the formation of the churches in Thessalonica and Corinth – was anchored to a historical figure, Jesus. This, in turn, is corroborated by notices appearing in Josephus and Tacitus about the connection of Christians with Christ, as noted earlier.[56]

Jesus in James, 1 Peter and Hebrews[57]

The technical rabbinic language of 'handing over' what the proclaimer had 'received' is peculiar to Paul among New Testament writers. This is no surprise; he had been trained in the Torah (and possibly its transmission) by the eminent Gamaliel.[58] Nevertheless, the letters of James, Hebrews and 1 Peter indicate that the churches associated with these leaders also arose from the proclamation of Jesus. Again, it is a historical figure to whom they refer.

The letter of James[59] appears to have been written relatively early. Its preference for 'works' over 'faith'[60] suggests that James

[56] See above, pp. 29–37.

[57] 2 Peter will not be reviewed in this study (but see 2 Pet. 1:14, 16–18). It comes after 1 Peter (2 Pet. 3:1), which letter amply illustrates the connection between the proclaimed word and the historical person, Jesus. No reference will be made to the letters of John because of the difficulties in establishing their date of writing.

[58] Acts 22:3. See M. Hengel, *The Pre-Christian Paul* (London: SCM, 1991), pp. 42–45.

[59] The identification of the author as 'James, a servant of God and of the Lord Jesus Christ' who is writing to 'the twelve tribes of the dispersion' makes it likely that he is the brother of the Lord and leader of the Jerusalem church. Jude introduces himself as 'a servant of Jesus Christ and brother of James'. The other noted James – James Zebedee – was killed in the early 40s (Acts 12:2).

[60] Jas. 2:14–26; *cf.* Gal. 2:15–21; Rom. 3:27 – 4:24.

was touching on issues raised by Paul in his letters to the Galatians and the Romans. James, therefore, probably wrote his letter some time after *c.* AD 55[61] and before his death in AD 62.

The connection between the proclaimed word and the historical person of Jesus noted in Paul's letters also holds true even in the letter of James. James writes to an explicitly Jewish[62] readership, using a 'wisdom' ethic and a relatively understated Christology and soteriology.[63] Nevertheless, he speaks of 'the word of truth' by means of which we become 'a kind of first fruits of his creatures',[64] and of those who 'hold the faith of the Lord Jesus Christ, the Lord of glory' as members of an assembly of believers.[65] To be sure, James makes no explicit reference to the person of the historical Jesus. There are, however, a number of ethical teachings which appear to echo the teachings of Jesus from a source which the gospel of Matthew seems to have employed.[66] Moreover, his reference to 'the wisdom . . . from above' and 'the righteous man' whom the Jews killed may be oblique references to Jesus, personified, as it were, as wisdom and righteousness.[67] In short, it is clear enough that those who became attached to Jesus through proclamation about him were given instruction in the teachings of the historical Jesus, and – in all likelihood – about his person as well.

The first letter of Peter lies within the time-frame *c.* AD 52–65. Silvanus, Peter's amanuensis, was with Paul in Corinth in the early 50s.[68] Peter was executed under Nero in about AD 65, according to Clement, writing thirty years later from Rome.[69] Can we be more precise? The letter's grim references to suffering fits with the aftermath of the fire in Rome in AD 64. Peter and his companions in Rome may have discerned ominous early signs pointing to developing hatred of Christians. When the fire broke out, destroying the greater part of the city,

---

[61] It is possible, however, that the 'faith' and 'works' controversy arose in the 40s, or even earlier, thus pre-dating the writing of Paul's letters.

[62] Jas. 1:1.

[63] *Cf.* J. Hartin, *James and the Q Sayings of Jesus* (Sheffield: JSOT, 1991).

[64] Jas. 1:18; *cf.* 1:22–23.   [65] Jas. 2:1–2.

[66] Jas. 1:17 (Mt. 7:11); Jas. 1:22–24 (Mt. 7:24); Jas. 2:10–11 (Mt. 5:19); Jas. 2:15 (Mt. 25:3); Jas. 3:6 (Mt. 12:36; 15:11); Jas. 4:11–12 (Mt. 7:1); Jas. 5:12 (Mt 5:34–37); Jas. 5:19–20 (Mt. 18:1). For a comprehensive list of parallels see J. B. Mayor, *The Epistle of James* (London, 1913), pp. lxxxv–xc.

[67] Jas. 3:15; 5:6.   [68] 2 Cor. 1:19; *cf.* 1 Pet. 5:12.   [69] *1 Clement* 5:1–4, 5.

the Christians were ready-made scapegoats.[70] They could be blamed for the fire; sufferings would be heaped upon them in Rome, and the shock-waves would reverberate upon Peter's readers in distant Asia Minor.[71]

Peter's letter is addressed to those who have been evangelized. Indeed, they have been 'born anew to a living hope' through the 'living . . . word of God' that had been proclaimed to them.[72] They are conscious, too, of their baptism, which presumably occurred at the time the gospel was declared to them.[73] This letter addresses the situation and circumstances in the aftermath of primary evangelism.

Equally, however, Peter alludes to the historical Jesus, under the rubric, 'the sufferings of Christ'.[74] He writes that Christ was 'made manifest at the end of the times' and that he 'suffered in the flesh', but that in those sufferings he did not sin by guileful, vengeful or threatening behaviour. His footprints they were to follow closely.[75] Peter writes to those who have not seen Christ, but as one who had himself seen Christ.[76] In 5:1 he addresses presbyters as a 'fellow presbyter and as a witness of the sufferings of Christ' (my translation). While these presbyters are fellow presbyters, they are not fellow witnesses. Only the writer, Peter, is a witness. The readers and their presbyters owe their relationship with Christ to the proclaimed message of Christ. But Peter had first-hand, physical knowledge of Christ. He had been a witness to the sufferings of Jesus.

Peter introduces this latter aspect of Jesus' life, in particular,

---

[70] Tacitus, *Annals* xv.44.   [71] 1 Pet. 1:6; 3:15, 17; 4:1, 7, 12–19; 5:6–10.

[72] 1 Pet. 1:3, 23, 25; *cf.* 1:12.   [73] 1 Pet. 3:21.

[74] 1 Pet. 1:11; 4:13; 5:1. The verb 'suffer' (*pathein*) occurs 13 times in 1 Peter, approximately half the occurrences in the NT. See R. H. Gundry, '*Verba Christi* in 1 Peter: Their Implications concerning the Authorship of 1 Peter and the Authenticity of the Gospel Tradition', *NTS* 13 (1966), pp. 336–350; 'Further Verb on *Verba Christi* in 1 Peter', *Bib* 55 (1974), pp. 211–232 (against E. Best, '1 Peter and the Gospel Tradition', *NTS* 16 (1969), pp. 95–113). J. O. Tuni, 'Jesus of Nazareth in the Christology of 1 Peter', *HJ* xxviii/3 (1987), pp. 292–304, draws a close connection between 'the sufferings of Christ', that is, of Jesus of Nazareth, and the 'good conduct' in the suffering of the Christian.

[75] 1 Pet. 1:20; 4:1; 2:21–23.

[76] 1 Pet. 1:8. Note the syntax of *hon ouk idontes agapate*: the aorist participle *idontes*, suggesting completed action; and the unexpected negative particle *ouk*, used normally with the indicative, not with participles. Although the readers had not seen Jesus, the writer had.

to strengthen the readers in their patient and non-retaliatory perseverance as Christians in the face of implacable hostility. The 'good' behaviour[77] of the Christian under suffering is to reflect and replicate the behaviour of Christ sustained under his sufferings. As with other writers who make reference to Jesus, the details are selected as appropriate to the circumstances of the readers; in particular, in their faithful witness to Jesus in circumstances of hostility. Such details are given no elaboration or justification. Evidently both writer and readers knew and accepted the underlying facts about Jesus to which the references apply.

The letter to the Hebrews is probably to be dated to the 60s.[78] The many references to the Jerusalem temple[79] imply that it was still in use, suggesting that the letter was written prior to AD 70, when the temple was destroyed. This appears to be confirmed by a reference to Timothy,[80] the younger contemporary of Paul. Timothy, who is known to the author and the readers, has just been released from prison, apparently in Italy,[81] where the author also appears to be at the time of writing. Timothy and the author intend to visit the readers, who, it is here suggested, were Christian Jews in Palestine. Perhaps Timothy had been imprisoned in Italy in the aftermath of the fire in Rome in AD 64 during Nero's pogrom against the Christians of Rome.

No letter in the New Testament so clearly proclaims the gospel on the one hand, and the reality of Jesus as a figure of history on the other, as does the letter to the Hebrews. The unknown author, who was not among the original followers of Jesus, writes as one who heard their proclamation.[82] That proclamation, a word which is 'living and active',[83] was accompanied by miracle signs and the gifts of the Holy Spirit.[84] (Perhaps the author was present in Jerusalem on the day of Pentecost when he heard the apostles first proclaim the risen Christ and when the Holy Spirit came in dramatic fashion.) He

[77] See 1:15; 2:12; 3:16; *cf.* 3:1–2.

[78] A majority of scholars posit a later dating for Hebrews. See *e.g.* W. G. Kümmel, *Introduction to the New Testament* (London: SCM, 1975), p. 403, for standard arguments.

[79] Heb. 5:1–4; 8:13; 9:6, 9; 10:1–3; 13:10–14.   [80] Heb. 13:23.

[81] Paul expected Timothy to come to him in Rome; 2 Tim. 4:9–13, 21.

[82] Heb. 2:1, 2, 4.   [83] Heb. 4:12.   [84] Heb. 2:4.

is deeply conscious that the gospel has come to him and those with him in circumstances of great power.[85]

This powerful sense of proclamation is tied to an equally strong sense of the historical Jesus. The author knows that Jesus was from the tribe of Judah, and therefore not a member of the priestly caste.[86] He writes, 'We see Jesus, who for a little while was made lower than the angels . . .' who 'partook' in 'flesh and blood' so as to be 'like his brethren in every respect'.[87] This Jesus was 'tempted in every way as we are, yet without sin', suggesting a knowledge of specific occasions of temptation faced and overcome by him.[88] He is a compassionate heavenly high priest who 'in the days of his flesh . . . offered up prayers and supplications, with loud cries and tears', and who 'learned obedience through what he suffered'.[89] We sense that, although he speaks in non-specific terms, both the writer and the readers know the circumstances of Jesus' sufferings. Again, without giving details, he refers to the hostility which Jesus suffered.[90] The author repeatedly writes of Jesus' obedience to God, expressed in his sacrificial death offered up for the salvation of others.[91]

As with Paul writing 2 Corinthians, the references are unsystematic and unsequential as well as selective, chosen from the various privations of Jesus to reinforce the message of the writer. The allusions to the historical Jesus emphasize his humanity and his perseverance in the face of sufferings for the very understandable reason that his readers needed to persevere in the face of grave difficulties at that time. His very lack of detail by way of elaboration suggests that both he and they knew about the circumstances of Jesus' sufferings. In short, this remarkable document reflects both the fact of the proclamation of the gospel which had come to them and a presumed knowledge of the historical Jesus.

Conclusion

Paul's earliest letters, but also James, 1 Peter and Hebrews, reflect the fact that the readers and their churches had become

---

[85] Heb. 2:4.   [86] Heb. 7:14.   [87] Heb. 2:7, 9–10, 14, 17.
[88] Heb. 4:15.   [89] Heb. 5:7–8.   [90] Heb. 12:2–3.
[91] *E.g.* Heb. 9:14; 10:5–10; 12:24.

believers because of the proclamation of the gospel. At the same time these letters reflect a knowledge of the historical Jesus to which the writer can appeal, and which the readers share. Strong backward links with Jesus' teaching as well as his death and resurrection are maintained. The information about Jesus that is presented is unsystematic, unsequential and selective, chosen on account of the perceived needs of the readers. In the case of the Corinthians Paul refers to Jesus to help them see the genuineness of a servant ministry as opposed to a triumphalist ministry, or a model of generosity when they are being tight-fisted. In the case of James's readers, Jesus is in the background as the wise teacher of godly behaviour. The readers of Hebrews and the believers of Asia Minor to whom Peter wrote are both pointed to Jesus' perseverance in suffering as encouragement for them in the face of strong opposition. Jesus, crucified and risen, was the impulse for the proclamation, but also its content. This word of proclamation is anchored to a genuinely historical person. The shadow of the historical Jesus, in particular his sufferings, lies across every page of these letters.

For the historian, the significance of the letters surveyed has several aspects. First, they are the earliest documents of Christianity, apparently pre-dating the more overtly biographical gospels. In the case of Paul, where the dating is secure, they are documents remarkable for their closeness in time to the historical Jesus. And they are written by one who had been part of Christian history almost from the outset, first as persecutor, then as apostle.

Secondly, they are quite close in time to the readers' own hearing of the gospel and their conversion. In the case of the Thessalonians and Corinthians, the time between their hearing the gospel and Paul's letters to them is known to have been brief. All that they know about Jesus has been acquired in a short space, either from Paul and his envoys in person (or, in the case of the Corinthians, from the Jewish missioners who attempted to infiltrate the churches).[92] It must be assumed, therefore, that Paul imparted information about Jesus when present with them.

Thirdly, since the letters are not evangelistic tracts, but issue-centred vehicles for reinforcement and correction, the historical information about Jesus which emerges must be regarded as

[92] 2 Cor. 11:4.

freely and innocently given, and therefore not in dispute. The more is this so because, as we have noted, it is unsystematic, unsequential and selective, according to the perceived needs of the readers.

Fourthly, it implies that scholars who seek to recover the historical Jesus must not omit the letters from their considerations, as they often do. Many reconstructed versions of Jesus are quite unlike the exalted figure whose proclamation was, as we have shown, presumed in the letters. Yet the one who was – to take Paul's account of his proclamation in 2 Corinthians – the Son of God, the Christ/Messiah and the Lord, was also humble in birth, a slave in ministry, meek and gentle in life, without sin and handed over for the sins of others in death. And God raised him from the dead.

Finally, the letters point to early and shared convictions of an exalted kind about Jesus. The non-evangelistic nature of the letters indicates that these convictions are shared by both writer and readers. The breadth of authorship of the letters – Paul, James, the writer to the Hebrews, Peter – each with constituent networks of congregations, shows how widespread, as well as early, were these shared convictions, even though we do not have certain details of the dating and precise authorship of all the letters. The brevity of the lead time between Jesus and the documentation of these convictions in the letters rules out theories of development and evolution. The most plausible – *historically* plausible – explanation of the early and exalted view of Jesus is the percussive impact of Jesus the Teacher, risen from the dead, upon his immediate followers, both before and after Easter.

One of the marks of modern Jesus-reconstructions is their discontinuity in a forwards direction. The reconstructed Jesus – apocalyptic prophet, devout Hasid, social reformer, Cynic gnomist, or whatever – never makes it on to sonship, messiahship or lordship in the mission preaching reflected in the letters. This Jesus begins and ends with himself. By contrast, continuity backwards towards the historical Jesus is the hallmark of the New Testament letters. The one who is proclaimed as Son of God, Christ and Lord is the same one, Jesus of Nazareth, the Teacher, now exalted, whose life, character, death and resurrection clearly emerge from the letters.

Unless historians of the New Testament take seriously the letters in regard to both the fact of proclamation and the connection of the proclaimed figure to the historical figure of Jesus, then the engine driving the New Testament from within – Jesus the Teacher who, as risen from the dead, was proclaimed as Jesus the Lord – will remain unrecognized. Failing to discern the inner dynamic which gives the New Testament story its impulse, scholars will continue to tinker at the edges, absorbed in background studies, social and psychological analyses and various forms of textual reconstructions, missing the action in the centre which explains everything. This is the logic of history.

Does the historical connection between Jesus of Nazareth and the proclaimed Christ matter theologically, as opposed to historically? Most assuredly it does.[93] His uniqueness and universal applicability are jeopardized by any attempt to cut the knot that ties them together. The proclaimed Christ is the self-same person, the Nazarene, the man of Galilee. The Christ was Jesus, the proclaimer, who, on account of his messiahship and sonship, through his resurrection, became the proclaimed. In this he is and always will be unique.

A proclaimed one who was historically rootless would be a mythic figure, providing for a merely mystical, obligation-free response, one lord among others. Because the Word was incarnate in Jesus of Nazareth, crucified and risen, God has made a full and final revelation and has truly reconciled the lost to himself. Nothing else and nothing less will do.

Excursus
Summary of information about Jesus
in the letters of Paul

The following information about Jesus can be found in the Pauline corpus.[94]

1. Jesus was a descendant of Abraham the patriarch.[95]

2. Jesus was a direct descendant of King David. This was a critical element in the belief that he was the Christ, the Messiah of Israel.[96]

---

[93] M. Kähler, *The So-Called Historical Jesus and the Historic Biblical Christ* (Philadelphia: Fortress, 1964), however, argued that Christian faith and a history of Jesus were, like oil and water, incompatible (p. 74).

[94] See also Wedderburn, 'Paul and the Story of Jesus', pp. 161–189.

[95] Gal. 3:16.   [96] Rom. 1:3; 9:5; 15:8; 1 Cor. 15:3.

3. Jesus 'born of *woman*' suggests that Paul knows of and confirms the virginal conception of Jesus.[97] Paul's words are in agreement with Matthew's: 'Mary, *of whom* Jesus was born, who is called Christ'.[98] Jesus was born of the woman, Mary, not of her husband Joseph.

4. Jesus was born and lived in poverty.[99]

5. Jesus was 'born under' and lived under Jewish law.[100]

6. Jesus had a brother named James, and other brothers, unnamed.[101]

7. His lifestyle was one of humility and meekness, agreeing with his words recorded in the gospel, 'I am gentle and lowly in heart'.[102]

8. He ministered primarily to Israel and Jews.[103]

9. He washed the feet of his disciples.[104]

10. He instituted a memorial meal on the night he was betrayed.[105]

11. He was cruelly treated at that time.[106]

12. He gave testimony before Pontius Pilate.[107]

13. He was killed by the Jews of Judea.[108] (References to his crucifixion[109] imply execution at Roman hands, on treasonable grounds.)

14. He was buried.[110]

15. He was raised on the third day and was seen alive on a number of occasions by many hundreds of witnesses, most of whom are still alive and, therefore, able to confirm this.[111]

---

[97] Paul's words in Gal. 4:4 appear to be connected in some way with material in the early chapters of the gospel of Luke: 'The time had fully come . . . to redeem' / 'God . . . has visited and redeemed his people . . . as he spoke by the mouth of his holy prophets' (Lk. 1:68–70); 'God sent forth his Son' / 'He . . . will be called Son of the Most High' (Lk. 1:32); 'born of woman' / 'Jesus . . . the son (as was supposed) of Joseph' (Lk. 3:23); 'born under the law' / 'according to [the] custom [of the law]' (Lk. 2:42). Was Paul familiar with a source which Luke subsequently incorporated in his gospel?

[98] Mt. 1:16. [99] 2 Cor. 8:9. [100] Gal. 4:4.

[101] Gal. 1:19; 1 Cor. 9:5. [102] 2 Cor. 10:1; Mt. 11:29.

[103] Rom. 15:8. [104] 1 Tim. 5:10. [105] 1 Cor. 11:23–25.

[106] Rom. 15:3. [107] 1 Tim. 6:13. [108] 1 Thes. 2:14–15.

[109] *E.g.* Gal. 2:20; 1 Cor. 1:16 – 2:2 *passim.* [110] 1 Cor. 15:4.

[111] 1 Cor. 15:4–6.

Chapter Four

Jesus in historical context

Social analysis

In this chapter I will seek to locate Jesus within the boundaries of his historical context. Here the question of historical outlook and method will be important. The Jesus studies of recent years have invested considerable research in the life and times of Galilee, with special interest directed to its sociology and economics.[1] Attention has been drawn to its indigenous villages, which were conservatively Jewish and relatively poor in comparison with the tetrarch's recently built cities, Sepphoris and (more recently) Tiberias, which, by contrast, were predominantly Gentile and wealthy. Moreover, it is argued, a rapid economic change had occurred owing to Herod Antipas's building programme and increased trading between Galilee and neighbouring Gentile regions. Consistent with a sociological approach, reference is made to the 'Jesus *movement*', along with the conviction that this 'movement' is able to be explained by a social-economic understanding of Galilee. Mack, Downing and Crossan see the movement led by Jesus as 'Cynic', espousing withdrawal from society. Freyne sees the movement as a positive model, based on traditional Jewish kinship models, as an alternative to those of the new foundations of Sepphoris and Tiberias.[2]

Here, however, there are several methodological problems. First, these authors do not begin with the extant documents closest to Jesus of Nazareth, seeking to understand him within

[1] For Galilee studies see S. Freyne, *Galilee from Alexander the Great to Hadrian: A Study of Second-Temple Judaism* (Wilmington: Glazier, 1980); L. I. Levine (ed.), *The Galilee of Late Antiquity* (Cambridge, MA: Harvard University Press, 1992); R. A. Horsley, *Galilee* (Valley Forge: Trinity, 1995).

[2] S. Freyne, 'The Geography, Politics and Economics of Galilee', in *Studying the Historical Jesus*, ed. B. Chilton and C. A. Evans (Leiden: Brill, 1994), p. 120.

his life and times. Rather, they begin with the Galilee context, as they reconstruct it, and then place the 'Jesus movement' within it, explaining the 'movement' by its social context. Secondly, this reconstructed sociology of Galilee is itself quite conjectural; the statistical data needed for social and economic analysis exist in fragmentary and incomplete form. Thirdly, when the gospel text (or an underlying source) is used, it is used selectively, as controlled by the social analysis, with passages presenting another view left out of account. Freyne himself comments that 'the quest for Jesus is rapidly becoming the quest for the historical Galilee'.[3]

Text-based attention to known individuals

Is there a more valid methodological approach to establishing a context for Jesus? In my view, a better process is to begin with extant documents, as near to the times as possible, which relate to known individuals, attempting to set them in their historical, religious, social and economic contexts. The gospel of Luke provides just such a context for Jesus; that is, the prophesyings of John the baptizer. John himself is given a quite precise historical reference. He began to prophesy in the fifteenth year of Tiberius, the emperor, when Pilate was governor of Judea and Herod (Antipas) tetrarch of Galilee, in the high-priesthood of Annas and Caiaphas.[4]

Jesus was circumscribed by these five persons. The rulership of Herod Antipas is the backdrop not only for Jesus' lifespan, but also for his Galilean ministry. John the baptizer was the immediate precursor of that ministry. The high priests and Pilate brought that ministry to its end in Jerusalem. In this regard, two highly significant facts must be noted. One is that each of these persons is referred to in sources outside the New Testament. The other is that these notable individuals were not merely there, forming a context, as it were. Jesus became involved with each of them, both indirectly and directly. Jesus was baptized by John in the Jordan, was tried by Caiaphas and Annas, interrogated by Herod Antipas and executed by Pilate in Jerusalem. These men and their activities are the context of Jesus and his activities.

[3] *Ibid.*, p. 76.   [4] Lk. 3:1–2.

What roles, then, are played by geography and archaeology? In my view these disciplines can provide useful sources, which, however, ought to be understood in the light of the texts. Landscape and architectural remains, by themselves, can tell us relatively little about history, but when considered alongside texts they can illuminate, confirm, modify or contradict those texts. Thus all that can be known about Galilee, Perea, Judea and Gentile regions visited by Jesus, whether by geography, archaeology or through the eyes of a near contemporary witness like Josephus, provides helpful illumination of historical texts.

Galilee studies – its geography, politics and history – are indeed helpful in providing commentary on the ministry of Jesus as found in the gospel texts. The land itself, its dominant lake in which fish are still to be found, the insulae and streetscape of Capernaum, the dense pattern of numerous village settlements dependent on a number of larger urban centres,[5] as well as the general surrounding topography of Galilee, establish an imaginable context for the ministry of Jesus.

Josephus, who gives a first-hand account of his military leadership in Galilee in the early years of the war against the invading Romans, is quite informative about the Galilee of that era. His narratives of his military campaigns in Galilee relate to a period only thirty or so years later than Jesus. The gospel of Mark also gives extensive information about the Gentile territories adjoining Galilee.[6] Mark's account of Jesus' ease of movement into and back from Gentile territories to the north and east fits well with the known circumstances of his era, but not with those of later times. In the years leading up to the outbreak of war in AD 66, Jew–Gentile relationships were to deteriorate dramatically, as for example in Caesarea Maritima. Mark's account of Jesus' travels to and ministry in Gentile

[5] D. Edwards, 'The Socio-Economic and Cultural Ethos of the Lower Galilee in the First Century: Implications for the Nascent Jesus Movement in the Galilee', in *The Galilee of Late Antiquity*, ed. L. I. Levine, pp. 53–73.

[6] The gospel of Mark, for example, refers precisely to the region (*chōra*) of the Gerasenes (5:1), the border (*ta horia*) of Tyre (7:24) and the villages (*kōmai*) of Bethsaida and Caesarea Philipppi (8:26–27). Mark's narrative and the parables of Jesus which appear in the synoptic gospels, with their references to villages, fields, market-places, fishing, casual labourers, absentee landlords and wealthy estate-owners, are consistent with our growing understanding of Galilee of the period. See A. N. Sherwin-White, *Roman Society and Roman Law in the New Testament* (Oxford: Oxford University Press, 1963), pp. 120–143.

territories is informed by the pre-war situation in Galilee, adding credibility to its historical authenticity.

The topography in and around Jerusalem is also of value in reconstructing Jesus' world. The extensive overlay of buildings in Jerusalem from the time of the Roman destruction of the city in AD 70 until today, however, makes that reconstruction difficult. Nevertheless, the Mount of Olives, the Kidron Valley, Gethsemane and Siloam are locations outside the still-standing Ottoman walls which can be visited and within which Jesus' activities can readily be imagined. Inside the walls the steady work of archaeology has made possible the recovery of a number of large mansions of the day, which may have been typical of the domiciles of high priests. Significant expanses of the walls of the temple mount are now exposed, as well as the street level of Herodian Jerusalem at a number of points.

Once again Josephus provides extensive eye-witness description of a location which is important in the ministry of Jesus. He was present with the Roman general Titus in the final stages of the siege and capture of the city, providing lengthy accounts of the disposition of the city and its temple. Much of the gospel of John, in particular, is set in and around Jerusalem. Impressive in this regard, for example, is John's reference to Aramaic place names, Bethzatha, Gabbatha and Golgotha, and to 'the portico of Solomon' in the temple where Jesus took shelter at the time of the Feast of Dedication, which falls in mid-winter.[7]

In short, within limits the reconstructed world of Galilee and Jerusalem is helpful in recovering the world of the historical Jesus. Knowledge of the Herodian power structures, the economic dynamism through markets open to neighbouring city states, the impact of the relocation of the Galilean capital from Sepphoris to Tiberias and the grandeur of mansions in Jerusalem all contribute something to the background landscape. But the geographical, architectural, political and socio-economic elements by themselves do not inform us about Jesus. In my view the cultural background, which is silent about Jesus, should not be taken as the dominant determinant leading to relegation of the gospel information, which has Jesus as its focus.[8] By that methodology a Jesus quite different from the Jesus of the gospels inevitably emerges.

[7] See Jn. 5:1; 19:13, 17; 10:22.   [8] See above, pp. 19–22.

Markers for the ministry of Jesus: Luke 3:1–2

We turn now to consider the five historically notable persons mentioned in Luke 3:1–2 who form the historical reference for Jesus' ministry and with each of whom he was involved.[9] These men were his context and he became, in different ways, connected with each of them. As they intersect with Jesus, these prominent men form 'markers' to his story. But more than that, the uncontrived and incidental nature of the references provides innocent testimony to the historical character of the gospel narratives.

John the baptizer

According to the four gospels the public ministry of Jesus followed immediately upon the ministry of John the baptizer.[10]

John the baptizer in the gospels and Josephus

The four gospels give considerable prominence to John the baptizer, referring to him almost ninety times. If for the moment we leave to one side the gospel references to John's role in relation to Jesus – that is, as forerunner and baptizer – the following details emerge. First, John baptized large numbers of Israelites in the Jordan River, apparently on the eastern or Perean side, within Antipas's jurisdiction, possibly to avoid trouble with the Romans who now controlled Judea.[11] Secondly,

---

[9] Luke had earlier indicated that both John and Jesus had been born during the reign of Herod, king of Judea, and that Jesus had been born at the time of a Roman census (Lk. 1:5, 2:1–2). Significantly, too, it is the historically minded Luke who gives the information that John's father, Zechariah, was a priest (of the division of Abijah); that his mother, Elizabeth, was also of the priestly line of Aaron; that Mary and Elizabeth were related (1:36); and that John was conceived in the days of Herod, king of Judea (1:5).

[10] For discussion on the various aspects of John the baptizer, with literature, see *DJG*, pp. 383–391. R. T. France, 'Jesus the Baptist?', in *Jesus of Nazareth: Lord and Christ*, ed. J. B. Green and M. Turner (Grand Rapids: Eerdmans, 1994), pp. 94–111, argues not only for continuity between John and Jesus, but, less convincingly, that Jesus pointedly continued to baptize throughout his ministry. For the proposal that Jesus was a disciple-protégé of John's and that he, too, baptized, see R. L. Webb, 'John the Baptist and his Relationship with Jesus', in *Studying the Historical Jesus*, ed. B. Chilton and C. A. Evans (Leiden: Brill, 1994), pp. 179–229.

[11] Jn. 1:28; 10:40. There is ample evidence from Josephus that the Roman authorities were concerned about charismatic prophetic figures. See further

---

John was believed to be a prophet.[12] His baptizing was in the context of his preaching to the people who came out to him in the wilderness.[13] It is specifically noted that John 'did no sign'.[14] Thirdly, John was imprisoned by the tetrarch of Galilee/Perea, and, at the request of the tetrarch's wife Herodias, beheaded.[15]

Josephus is the other source of information about John. He devotes a paragraph to 'John surnamed the Baptist'.[16] The three points noted above in the synoptic gospels are also to be found in Josephus. There are differences, however. First, Josephus does not specify the Jordan River as the location for John's baptizing. Secondly, Josephus supplies the name of the prison as Machaerus, located in Perea overlooking the Dead Sea. Thirdly, whereas the gospels[17] attribute John's arrest and execution to his rebuke of the tetrarch for his marriage to the wife of a brother still alive, Josephus states that it was due to Antipas's fear of John's popularity and the possibility of an uprising led by him.[18]

Fourthly and most significant of all, however, is the synoptic gospels' apocalyptic mode of description of John, as opposed to Josephus' non-apocalyptic description. This is typical of Josephus, who regularly translates such elements within Judaism into political or philosophical ones, as, for example, in his portrayal of the Pharisees, the Sadducees, the Essenes and the revolutionaries as 'four philosophies'. Thus, whereas in Matthew John preached repentance in face of the approaching kingdom of God, in Josephus John exhorted the people 'to live righteous lives, to practise justice towards their fellows and piety towards

---

P. W. Barnett, 'The Jewish Sign Prophets – AD 40–70: Their Intentions and Origin', *NTS* 27 (1981), pp. 679–697. For the argument that John's baptizing activities also occurred in Batanea, see R. Riesner, 'Bethany Beyond the Jordan (John 1:28): Topography, Theology and History in the Fourth Gospel', *TB* 38 (1987), pp. 29–63.

[12] Mk. 11:32.   [13] Mt. 3:1–10; Lk. 3:7–14.

[14] Jn. 10:41. Moreover, Josephus does not mention any signs associated with John the baptizer.

[15] The gospel of John is silent about John's death; Luke does not attribute it to Herodias's influence.

[16] *Antiquities* xviii.116–119.

[17] While the gospel of John gives no reason for John's arrest, a degree of hostility towards him from the religious establishment in Jerusalem is suggested by their interrogation of him (Jn. 1:19–29; 4:1).

[18] Nevertheless, Josephus knows about Antipas's divorce of his Nabatean wife and his remarriage to Herodias (*Antiquities* xviii.103, 113).

God.' There can be no question, however, but that the gospels have the correct emphasis. Josephus's preacher of morality must be made to fit in with the gospels' truer picture of the prophet of Yahweh's impending kingdom and judgment.[19]

These four differences are not contradictions, but variations of emphasis and detail arising from the writers' own viewpoints and interests. When the synoptic gospels and Josephus are looked at side by side they provide a coherent account of the public ministry of John the baptizer.[20] Since John began to prophesy in Tiberius's 'fifteenth year' (c. AD 28), and was imprisoned soon after Jesus' first Passover in Jerusalem[21] (probably AD 30),[22] that ministry lasted about two years.[23] John the baptizer was, then, a significant historical figure who forms a clear marker for the ministry of Jesus of Nazareth. Moreover, the context provided by John's activities also enhances our sense of the historical probity of the gospels' account of the relationship of Jesus to John.

John's message

As noted above, John's message was powerfully eschatological. Yahweh was soon to act, bringing his kingdom and judgment. Like the prophets to Israel whom God raised up at earlier times, John called upon the people to repent, that is, to turn back to Yahweh their covenant God. The people were far from God; despite their confidence in it, their biological descent from Abraham would be to no avail. Yahweh's axe was raised against

---

[19] Matthew's account of John's ministry (3:1–12) is likely to be historically accurate. The failure of a fiery apocalyptic fulfilment of his words is itself evidence of their veracity.

[20] It is noted, however, that the synoptics and John give different impressions of Jesus' involvement with the baptizer. The synoptics imply that Jesus' ministry began only when John was imprisoned, that is, their ministries were 'back to back'. John's more expansive account suggests that the ministries of the two men overlapped for a period (see Mk. 1:14; Mt. 4:12–13; Lk. 3:18–23; cf. Jn. 3:22–24; 4:1–2).

[21] Cf. P. L. Maier, 'The Date of the Nativity and the Chronology of Jesus' Life', in Chronos, Kairos, Christos, ed. J. Vardaman and E. M. Yamauchi (Winona Lake: Eisenbrauns, 1989), p. 120, who estimates that the duration of John's public activities was six to nine months. However, Josephus's attribution of divine vengeance to Antipas's defeat by Aretas in AD 37/38 (that is, some eight or so years later) gives some indication of John's reputation and influence, implying a ministry of some duration greater than six to nine months.

[22] Jn. 3:24; 4:43; cf. Mk. 1:14.   [23] See the excursus on pp. 111–114.

them. If the fruits of repentance were not forthcoming, all would be lost in the coming fiery judgment.

John's demand that penitent Jews enter the waters of baptism as a sign of their return to Yahweh was radical, an assault on their sense of holy nationhood. Baptism was an initiatory rite of passage to Judaism for *Gentiles!*[24] By his demand that the people be baptized, John may have been saying to a self-satisfied people that they were no better than Gentiles, so radical was their need to return to Yahweh their God.

Perhaps, too, this prophet-baptizer's priestly descent, and his experience of the temple and its practices, influenced his call to the people. Was his promise of forgiveness upon repentance and baptism a prophetic protest against a current dependence upon the temple and its sacrifices as atonement for sins?[25] Further, John's cultic background may have influenced his salutation of Jesus as the Lamb of God bearing the sins of the world.[26] In turn, that same insight into current cultic practices in Jerusalem may explain Jesus' curse of the fig tree and the subsequent assault on the merchants in the temple.

Unlike Josephus, the gospels make a direct connection between the covenantal 'turning' of the people and baptism. The gospels see in this 'return' of the people of Yahweh a fulfilment of the oracle of Malachi (and Isaiah).[27] These prophets foresaw a 'messenger' of Yahweh who was to prepare the 'way for Yahweh'. The gospel writers see this 'way' as a *people* made ready by John for Yahweh's intervention by means of the coming 'mightier one'.

It is likely that John had a prophet's consciousness that he was preparing a remnant people for Yahweh's intervention by means of one who was to come.[28] But he also appears to have been conscious of his role in the recognition of an *elect individual*

[24] See T. W. Manson, *The Servant Messiah* (Cambridge: Cambridge University Press, 1961), pp. 43–45.

[25] Webb, 'John the Baptist', p. 197.

[26] Jn. 1:29. Most, however, take the baptizer's words to be those of the evangelist, and therefore historically anachronistic. There is extended discussion in R. E. Brown, *The Gospel According to John* 1 (London: Chapman, 1966), pp. 58–63.

[27] Mal. 3:1; Is. 40:3.

[28] Some argue that in their presentations the evangelists are seeking to demote John in relation to later, more exalted, views of Jesus (for discussion see *e.g.* G. N. Stanton, *The Gospels and Jesus*, Oxford: Oxford University Press, 1989,

from among the people. 'For this I came baptizing,' the fourth evangelist records him as saying, '. . . that *he* might be revealed to Israel.'[29] In the course of baptizing the people of Israel, John recognized and identified Jesus as that Israelite upon whom the Spirit had come, who would pour out his Spirit upon the people.

In prophesying the coming of a human instrument of Yahweh's kingdom and judgment, John may have created the impression that he was that instrument. But John insisted that he was not that one. Across the sources underlying the gospels there is impressive agreement that John spoke of 'a mightier one' who was to come after him, whose sandals he was not worthy to untie.[30] In strongly eschatological terms John specifically contrasted his own baptism with water with the baptism with the Holy Spirit by the coming 'mightier one'.

On historical grounds one must conclude that John was the immediate precursor of Jesus. More fundamentally, however, by his prophesying and baptizing John saw himself as preparing the 'way for the Lord', that is, a remnant people for Yahweh's 'mighty one'. Further, it seems likely that by these activities John recognized Jesus as that Israelite who was the Spirit-anointed one who would fulfil the end-time purposes of Yahweh. We can only speculate as to the place John's ministry had in Jesus' own sense of God's calling and commissioning of him. It may have been significantly greater than we have thought.

Jesus' verdict on John the baptizer
Jesus' connection with John and opinion of him occur at various places in the (synoptic) gospels, but especially in Matthew 11:2–19. John and the tetrarch are not merely part of the landscape background to Jesus. Jesus is connected with John, who in turn is connected with Herod Antipas.

Jesus is recorded as having sent an answer back to John in prison by several of the baptizer's disciples whom he had sent to

---

pp. 98–99, 165–169). On the contrary, the synoptics give a very high profile to John, both as the successor of the OT prophets and in their record of Jesus' testimony to John, neither of which would have appeared had the evangelists set out to diminish the baptizer's role. John, for his part, while insisting that the baptizer is 'a man sent by God' (Jn. 1:6), none the less portrays him as a humble witness to the 'Lamb of God' (1:19–29). Yet John does not gloss over the tension implicit in the two baptizing groups (Jn. 3:22 – 4:1).

[29] Jn. 1:31.   [30] Mk. 1:7–8; Mt. 3:11; Lk. 3:16; Jn. 1:27; *cf.* Acts 13:25.

Jesus. In effect, Jesus assents to the proposition that he is the one who was to come. Jesus then reminds the listening crowds why they had gone out to John in the wilderness. It was to see a great prophet; indeed, the one Malachi foretold as preparing the way of Yahweh. In what is probably a tilt at the tetrarch of Galilee-Perea who has imprisoned John, Jesus says that the people had not gone to the wilderness to see a mere reed shaken by the wind or a courtier wearing soft clothes in a king's palace. In texts which, because of their vivid words, can scarcely be doubted, Jesus ties himself into a triangular relationship with John and the tetrarch. John is the one who 'fore-ran' Jesus; next to John, Herod Antipas is a mere 'reed', a man in soft clothing in a king's palace.

Moreover, Matthew records a rather puzzling statement, to the effect that in the time since John began to prophesy – that is, for about two years – 'the kingdom of heaven has suffered violence, and men of violence take it by force'. Clearly this is a historical statement describing historical events. But to what is Jesus referring? It could be a reference to the tetrarch's violent seizure of John, prophet and baptizer; or (more probably) Jesus could be referring metaphorically to sinners' access into the kingdom of God, as a result of his teaching.[31] Most probably of all, however, Jesus is alluding to the rise of religious and nationalistic zeal which John's eschatological prophesyings had stirred up, including among Jesus' own followers.[32] Whatever the explanation, it cannot be doubted that Jesus is referring to a particular historical situation which had been precipitated by John's activities and, quite probably, those of Jesus as well.

Conclusion
John the baptizer is well attested within the gospels and by an interesting parallel statement in Josephus. John is of great importance in establishing a precise historical context for the beginnings of the ministry of Jesus. The manner of Jesus' references, however, indicates that John is not merely a

[31] *Cf.* Lk. 16:16.
[32] See P. W. Barnett, 'Who were the BIASTAI?' *RTR* xxxvi.3 (1977), pp. 67–70; D. A. Carson, 'Do the Prophets and the Law Quit Prophesying before John? A Note on Matthew 11:13', in *The Gospels and the Scriptures of Israel*, ed. C. A. Evans and W. R. Stegner, *JSNT* Supplement Series 104 (Sheffield: Sheffield Academic Press, 1995), pp. 179–194.

backdrop to Jesus; Jesus is connected to John in a definite way.

Herod Antipas

Closely connected with John the baptizer in another way was Herod Antipas, who was responsible for the imprisonment and killing of John in the dungeon at Machaerus in Perea, overlooking the Dead Sea. Herod Antipas is of particular importance for any enquiry into Jesus. He became tetrarch[33] of Galilee-Perea in 4 BC, a short time after Jesus' birth (probably in 5 BC), and continued to rule that region until his exile in AD 39, about six years after the crucifixion of Jesus. His period of rule forms a backdrop to the entire span of Jesus' life. Moreover, since Herod Antipas[34] was the ruler of Galilee where the greater part of Jesus' ministry was exercised, he is of special interest for Jesus studies. Fortunately we have extensive information[35] about the man whom Jesus called 'that fox'.

Herod, tetrarch of Galilee-Perea[36]

After the death of Herod 'the Great' in 4 BC there were serious uprisings throughout the realm, including the territories of

[33] A 'tetrarch' was, literally, 'a ruler of a fourth' part of a kingdom or region. Augustus appointed Antipas and Philip as tetrarchs to rule over smaller sections of Herod's now sub divided realm, with Archelaus appointed as ethnarch to rule a rather larger region.

[34] 'Herod' became a dynastic title which Antipas appears to have used after Archelaus's exile in AD 6.

[35] On Herod Antipas, with literature, see H. Hoehner, *Herod Antipas* (Grand Rapids: Zondervan, 1980), and *DJG*, pp. 322–324.

[36] The synoptic gospels provide two kinds of information about Herod Antipas, the official and the personal. First, these sources provide information about his *official* position. According to Mark he is 'King Herod', whereas both Matthew and Luke, with greater precision, call him 'Herod the tetrarch' (Mk. 6:14; Mt. 14:1; Lk. 3:1; 9:7; Acts 13:7; *cf.* Mt. 14:9). For his part Luke knows that Galilee is 'Herod's jurisdiction' (Lk. 23:6). Matthew and Mark are aware that Herod Antipas seized and imprisoned John over the prophet's admonitions regarding the marriage to Herodias (Mk. 6:17–18; Mt. 14:3). All three synoptics mention that Antipas had John beheaded in prison. But, secondly, the gospels give us some understanding of Antipas's *character* and of the nature of his administration. What is the source of this information? The original disciples of Jesus on whom the gospels depend, directly or indirectly, were Galileans and therefore aware of life in the tetrarchy. Inside information about the tetrarch would also have been available to these disciples through Joanna, wife of Antipas's steward, Chusa. Moreover, Manaen, the former courtier of Herod the tetrarch, subsequently

Galilee and Perea which Antipas was to rule. Only the intervention of the Roman legions from Syria restored peace and order to the territories. On assuming his tetrarchy, Antipas set about rebuilding and re-fortifying the cities which the insurgents had recently destroyed: Sepphoris in Galilee and Betharamphtha in Perea. Like his father, Antipas knew well the strategic importance of fortified places. Antipas did not, however, deem either city as suitable for the seat of government; so in AD 17 he set about planning and building an entirely new city on the western side of the Lake of Galilee, where there were hot springs. He named it Tiberias after the emperor who had succeeded Augustus three years earlier. Planned on Hellenistic lines and with Hellenistic political and educational institutions, Antipas's new city gravely offended Jewish scruples, erected as it was on a burial ground. Antipas's palace was decorated with idolatrous effigies and opulently furnished; the majority of the citizens were Gentiles. A few years later, when war with Rome broke out (AD 66), the local Galileans showed their revulsion for Antipas's establishment by demolishing this palace with its blasphemous decorations and plundering its luxuries. As noted earlier in relation to John the baptizer, Jesus' mention of 'a reed shaken by the wind' and a man clothed in soft clothing, such as live in kings' houses, probably referred to the tetrarch Antipas domiciled at Tiberias in luxurious quarters beside a lake where reeds grew.[37]

There is no record in the gospels indicating that Jesus visited Tiberias (or Sepphoris) during the course of his public ministry.[38] Presumably it would have been dangerous to do so. Perhaps Jesus made Capernaum the centre of his ministry

---

came to be a prophet in the church in Syrian Antioch, the home of Luke the historian, author of the two-volume work covering the life and ministry of Jesus and the progress of the witness to Christ from Jerusalem to Rome.

[37] For the view that the reeds on Antipas's coinage struck at Tiberias relate to the reeds of the Lake of Galilee at Tiberias, which Jesus' dismissive remark in Mt. 11:11 associates with the tetrarch, see G. Theissen, *The Gospels in Context: Social and Political History in the Synoptic Tradition* (Edinburgh: T. and T. Clark, 1992), pp. 25–42.

[38] S. Freyne, 'Urban–Rural Relationships in First-Century Galilee: Some Suggestions from the Literary Sources', in *The Galilee of Late Antiquity*, ed. L. I. Levine, pp. 75–91, states that 'Jerusalem, not the Hellenistic cities [in and near the Galilee] had the controlling influence over the majority [of the rural] population' (p. 81).

because he could easily slip across the borders of Gaulanitis, out of reach of the tetrarch. But there can be little doubt that Jesus knew about life in the Galilean capital. It was, after all, a mere ten miles down the lake from Capernaum, a large city and in full view, a constant visual reminder of the Herodian ruler and his menacing power.

The gospels give some hints of the inner workings of Antipas's tetrarchy. Present at Antipas's birthday banquet where John would be beheaded were the three élite groups of his establishment: administrators or 'chief officials' (*megistanes*, 'great ones'), army commanders (*chiliarchoi*, colonels) and estate-owners who were civic leaders (*prōtoi*, 'chief men').[39]

In regard to 'chief men', Josephus mentions a faction in Tiberias composed of 'respectable citizens', included among whom were several named Herod, who were evidently members of the royal house.[40] Josephus also refers to the ten 'chief men' (*prōtoi*, the same term used in Mark 6:21) who were the executive committee of the city council (*boulē*) of Tiberias.[41] Probably the 'chief men' were the wealthy landowners who dominated the civic and political life in Tiberias and other large towns, and who formed Antipas's court.

This reference may throw light on that mysterious group whom Mark calls 'Herodians'.[42] The élite group who were present at Antipas's birthday banquet most likely approximate to the Herodians. They were dependent upon his patronage; he needed their support. It is possible that they sought to fulfil wider aspirations for their Herod, namely, the restoration of Herodian rule to the former king's realm, that is, the whole of Palestine. This would mean the removal of Roman provincial rule of Judea.

The gospels and Acts hint that various people connected with the tetrarch were touched by Jesus' ministry in Galilee. The 'royal official'[43] who approached Jesus in Cana about his sick son was probably a military or civil administrator serving the tetrarch in Capernaum, a significant border town. Also from Capernaum was the centurion, a Gentile military officer serving there in Antipas's military forces, possibly on secondment from Roman legionary services, who sought healing for his

---

[39] *Tois megistasin kai tois chiliarchois* (Mk. 6:21).   [40] *Life*, p. 33.
[41] *Ibid*, pp. 296, 67, 313, 381.   [42] Mk. 3:6; 12:13.   [43] *Basilikos* (Jn. 4:46).

attendant.[44] Levi/Matthew, a customs official employed by the tetrarch in Capernaum to collect tolls on the great trunk road that passed nearby joining Mesopotamia to Egypt, left his post to join Jesus' group of followers. Such a 'tax collector' in Galilee was not a privatized contractor, as was Zacchaeus in a Roman jurisdiction; Levi/Matthew was a bureaucrat in Antipas's Galilee.[45]

A more direct connection between Jesus and the tetrarch's circle must have existed with Joanna. Her husband, Chusa, was Antipas's domestic steward or estate manager (*epitropos*).[46] Joanna accompanied Jesus and, with other women, provided for the disciples during their ministry in Galilee. Jesus had healed Joanna and Mary from Magdala – a town on the lakeside a few miles to the north of Tiberias – 'of evil spirits and infirmities'.[47] Joanna and Mary were evidently closely connected with Jesus. They were present with him in Jerusalem at the time of the crucifixion. They were among the women who, on coming to anoint the body of Jesus after the Sabbath, found the tomb empty.[48] The wife of one of Antipas's closest associates was a witness to the empty tomb, and therefore almost certainly to the resurrection.

More significant again among Antipas's entourage was his close friend (and probable court-member, *syntrophos*),[49] Manaen (= Menahem), who in the 40s was one of the prophets and teachers in the church in Syrian Antioch.[50] As one of the tetrarch's *prōtoi*, 'chief men', Manaen may have been present at the fateful banquet in Perea when John was beheaded. Perhaps Joanna had spoken to Manaen about Jesus.

Galilee under Herod the tetrarch
As a client ruler of the Romans Herod was allowed to raise an income of 200 talents from his territories.[51] The tetrarch raised this, together with tribute payable to Rome, by means of various

---

[44] Mt. 8:5–13; Lk. 7:1–10.
[45] See Freyne, 'The Geography, Politics and Economics of Galilee', p. 103.
[46] Alternatively, he may have been foreman of an estate or estates (*cf.* Josephus, *Antiquities* xviii.194).
[47] Lk. 8:2.   [48] Lk. 24:10.
[49] Literally 'nourished with'. *Syntrophos* can mean 'boyhood friend' or 'intimate friend'.
[50] Acts 13:1.   [51] Josephus, *War* ii.95; *Antiquities* xvii.318.

forms of taxation, levied locally and paid in kind. These taxes included land tax, poll tax, levies for building projects (such as for the rebuilding of Sepphoris and the building of Tiberias) and customs tax on goods moved from one district to another. In addition there was a half-shekel tax payable by all Jews for the upkeep of the temple.[52] Taxes in Antipas's Galilee were collected by officials employed by the tetrarch; tax contracting by *publicani* or private agents appears to have been restricted to the Roman jurisdiction.[53] Levi/Matthew the *telōnēs* (customs official) was not a private tax contractor but one of Antipas's officials, part of his bureaucracy.

Such taxes, however, were unevenly levied. A remark made in passing by Jesus suggests the Herodian privileged circle may have paid little or no tax. 'What do you think, Simon?' Jesus asked. 'From whom do the kings of the earth take toll or tribute? From their sons or from others?' When Simon replied, 'From others,' Jesus said, 'Then the sons are free.'[54] The aristocrats who held large landholdings appeared to pay no tax.

There is some evidence that peasant farmers typically had no reserves of produce for the payment of land and poll tax in the event of failed crops, drought or other misadventure.[55] It is known that debt records were held in Sepphoris;[56] presumably mortgaging of landholdings was commonplace. Some of the day labourers as described in Jesus' parable of the workers in the vineyard had probably lost their lands through the combination of inexorable taxes and misadventure.[57] Jesus' advice to settle before being taken to court, rather than risk imprisonment, may also be set against a background of debt litigation against peasant farmers in financial difficulty.[58]

Based on the gospels and Josephus, it appears that Galilee was a pyramidal social-economic structure. The pinnacle was the

[52] Mt. 17:24–27.

[53] Freyne, 'The Geography, Politics and Economics of Galilee', pp. 101–104, argues that Jesus' endorsement of tax collectors was offensive, not because they were social outcasts, but because they were bracketed with prostitutes, as part of the promiscuous environment of the tetrarchy.

[54] Mt. 17:25–26.

[55] The Galilean leaders (*prōtoi*) anticipated that the agricultural strike over Caligula's threat to desecrate the temple would lead to banditry, since the striking peasants would not have the wherewithal to pay their taxes. See *War* ii.184–203; *Antiquities* xviii.261–309.

[56] Josephus, *Life* 38; *War* ii.247; vi:354.   [57] Mt. 20:1–16.   [58] Mt. 5:25–26.

tetrarch and the small Herodian élite, *megistanes, chiliarchoi* and *prōtoi*. Beneath the pinnacle were bureaucrats, attendants, tax collectors, officials and lesser military who held the structure in place. As noted already, some of these came into contact with Jesus. Beneath them was a relatively small class of those who managed to retain their land – self-employed farmers, artisans and fishermen – represented by Joseph the *tektōn* (builder), the father of the prodigal in the parable and the fishing partners in Capernaum. Several of these even had hired employees. Jesus and his group appear not to have been at the bottom of the social heap. At the base of the pyramid were the numerous landless folk, driven from their holdings by unforgiving taxes and misfortune. Their properties will have been absorbed into estates of the privileged élites.

The moral watchdogs of the populace were the Pharisees, who exercised their influence through the synagogues. The ministry of Jesus attracted the attention of pharisaic leaders from Jerusalem, who visited Galilee to confront the new prophet.[59] After all, Galilee had been brought back again under the covenant only in Hasmonean times. It lay beyond apostate Samaria, vulnerable to syncretism. Moreover, it was 'Galilee of the Gentiles', surrounded to the east, north and west by Gentile city states and bisected by the great Via Maris with its multitude of travellers. Galilee was subject to influences not experienced in Judea.

Antipas was tetrarch of Galilee-Perea for forty-three years (4 BC–AD 39). According to Josephus, the tetrarch 'loved his tranquillity'.[60] During his era Galilee was opened up to greater trading with Tyre and the other Hellenstic city states. Moreover, there had been considerable city rebuilding and building by him, respectively Sepphoris in 3 BC and Tiberias in AD 17. The construction of Tiberias began a decade before Jesus commenced his public ministry in Galilee.

The proposal that these economic forces destabilized Galilee, thus providing for the rise of Jesus as a social reformer, appears quite fanciful.[61] If a destabilizing factor is sought as a catalyst for Jesus' ministry, one need look no further than the cluster of

[59] Mk. 3:22; 7:1.   [60] *Antiquities* xviii.245.
[61] So Freyne, 'The Geography, Politics and Economics of Galilee', pp. 116–121.

events which occurred in the late 20s. The flight back to Petra by Antipas's wife, a Nabatean princess, was followed by Antipas's marriage to his brother's wife.[62] This provoked the denunciations of John the baptizer, which in turn led the tetrarch to imprison and later to behead this highly regarded prophet. These events, more than conjectural socio-economic circumstances, created a climate of expectation in which Jesus was given a ready hearing by the people of Galilee, some of whom had been disciples of John. Among them were some who would become followers of Jesus.

In short, the gospel and Acts, when read with Josephus, provide a historical setting for Jesus' ministry in Galilee. We catch glimpses of the ruling élite of the tetrarchy, who are probably closely connected with the Herodians. We see members of the tetrarch's household and court, as well as lower-level officials. Again, however, we not only see the context, but we observe that Jesus is part of that context. He heals an official's son. He is followed by Joanna, the wife of Chusa, steward or estate-manager of the tetrarch. And Levi, the border-customs official of Capernaum, became one of the twelve, who would one day write a gospel.

Herod the tetrarch and Jesus
There are several passages in the gospels and Acts which point to the interlocking historical connections between Jesus and Herod the tetrarch.[63]

Mark 6:14 and parallels. After some time ministering in Galilee, Jesus initiated the mission of the twelve disciples to the towns of Galilee. It must have seemed to the tetrarch that the charismatic populist, Jesus, had multiplied his labours twelvefold! Even if the twelve did not actually preach in each of the 204 towns of Galilee,[64] their activities were certainly sufficiently extensive to come to the attention of the tetrarch.[65] He concluded that the twelve were an extension of the ministry of Jesus, who, he

---

[62] *Antiquities* xviii.103, 113.

[63] This is not to suggest that such references are to be accepted naïvely, at face value. It is not a matter of casting doubt over a particular reference so much as prudently recognizing that the biblical writers, like others in every era, have their own points to make. Their overall redactional interests need to be assessed as part of the historian's craft.

[64] Josephus, *Life* 235.   [65] Mt. 14:13; Mk. 6:14; Lk. 9:9.

surmised, was John the baptizer now somehow alive again and active within his jurisdiction. The tetrarch was upset that, having beheaded John, his works were being replicated on a grand scale in his territory. Evidently Jesus discerned great danger to himself in the tetrarch's agitation.[66]

John 6:1–15/Mark 6:30–46.[67] The next event – the Galilean attempt to make Jesus king – is closely connected with the situation just described. The mission of the twelve ended, a great crowd from the towns visited by the twelve now converged on Jesus and the twelve. Whether inadvertently or deliberately, the mission of the twelve in the towns had aroused powerful eschatological expectations among the people of Galilee. With the crowd assembled before him, and hungry, Jesus fed them with the loaves and fishes.

John's account reaches its climax with the Galileans seeking to make Jesus their king, a conclusion entirely consistent with Mark's version of the frenetic 'running together' of the people beforehand from all the towns to meet Jesus.[68] This 'messianic uprising', as H. W. Montefiore called it,[69] can hardly have escaped the attention of the tetrarch of Galilee sitting in his palace in Tiberias just across the waters of the Galilean lake! The immense popularity of John had been revisited upon him in the person of another prophet. Perhaps the tetrarch brooded on the fact that the higher authorities had not seen fit to make *him* a king, whereas the people were ready to bestow that honour first on John and now on Jesus!

Be that as it may, according to what we can infer from Mark, Jesus did not again appear publicly in Galilee after this incident.

[66] Mt. 14:13.

[67] Mark and John give the most extensive accounts, each telling his story with his own emphasis. For Mark, Jesus is the compassionate shepherd-king feeding the people with an abundance of peasant fare in contrast with the orgy of a cruel and drunken king during which the righteous prophet John is beheaded. The fourth evangelist, on the other hand, relates his narrative to underscore Jesus as all-knowing and all-powerful in contrast with the disciples in their helpless unbelief.

[68] Remarkably, however, Mark omits altogether the climactic king-making attempt of the Galileans. Perhaps he passes over this treasonable detail out of consideration for a Roman readership who might be alarmed to think that the founder of this new movement could incite such social disruption in his homeland.

[69] 'Revolt in the Desert?' *NTS* 8 (1962), pp. 135–141.

Rather, Jesus now travelled extensively in neighbouring Gentile territories to the north, north-east, north-west and east of Galilee. It may not be a coincidence that the disciples declare Jesus to be 'the Christ' at Caesarea Philippi, outside Antipas's jurisdiction.[70] The historicity of these journeys away from danger at the hands of the tetrarch can scarcely be doubted. The politics and the geography dovetail neatly.

In his final journey to Jerusalem, Jesus was forced to travel through Perea, Antipas's other territory, where he faced two threatening situations.[71] First, *Mark 10:2*. His pathway to Jerusalem by way of Samaria blocked, as it ordinarily was to Galileans coming to Jerusalem, Jesus diverted across the Jordan into Perea. Jesus was now in the 'wilderness' where John prophesied and baptized. The Pharisees' test question, 'Is it lawful for a man to put away a wife?' (my translation), was full of menace. The tetrarch had done precisely that, in the face of the admonitions of the prophet of Perea, John the baptizer. The Nabatean princess had passed through that territory in her clandestine flight back to her father in his desert kingdom beyond the mountains. John had been beheaded for his troubles at nearby Machaerus. Jesus' reply was as unequivocal as the repeated oracle of John the baptizer's, saying in effect, 'It is not lawful.'[72]

Secondly, *Luke 13:31–35*. In another Perean incident Jesus was again approached by Pharisees, on this occasion sympathetic to him. 'Get away from here,' they warned, 'for Herod wants to kill you.' Jesus replied, 'Go and tell that fox . . .' In these words are to be found Jesus' assessment of the ruler in whose territory he had laboured. To Jesus Herod was a mere reed shaken by the wind, a man in soft clothing living in a palace,[73] and a 'fox', one characterized by cunning yet with a sense of inferiority.[74] By contrast, for his part, Jesus would not be deterred from finishing his course. He would go on to Jerusalem although he knew that certain death awaited him there.

Luke 23:6–12. In Jerusalem at Jesus' final Passover the two men eventually met.[75] The temple authorities brought Jesus to

[70] Mk. 8:29.   [71] Lk. 9:51–56.   [72] See Mk. 10:3–9.

[73] Mt. 11:7–8.

[74] See Hoehner, *Herod Antipas*, pp. 343–347, who points out that the fox as inferior was sometimes contrasted with the lion's greatness.

[75] *Cf.* M. L. Soards, 'Tradition, Composition and Theology in Luke's

the Roman governor, accusing him of treason and political agitation 'from Galilee even to this place' (verse 5). Hearing that his prisoner belonged to Herod's jurisdiction, Pilate sent Jesus off to the tetrarch, hoping, perhaps, to be relieved of a difficult decision. According to Luke, the tetrarch had 'long desired to see' Jesus, having heard about him, in particular in regard to his miracles. Doubtless such information in regard to the miracles of Jesus and the twelve had been brought to the tetrarch by the Herodians and their spies, and perhaps, too, by his steward Chusa, whose wife Joanna Jesus had healed.[76]

Jesus was silent before the tetrarch's interrogation, so he sent him back to Pilate. Antipas may have been as unwilling as Pilate to take responsibility for disposing of Jesus. Having borne the opprobrium of the people for his treatment of John the baptizer, the ever-'fox'-like tetrarch was probably relieved that Jesus had been arrested in Jerusalem, where the Romans had jurisdiction.

Conclusion

The gospels, Acts and Josephus (with some data from Philo)[77] provide extensive information about the ruler in whose tetrarchy Jesus was raised, where John baptized, preached and was beheaded, and where the greater part of Jesus' public ministry was conducted. In particular, we note that Antipas was appointed as tetrarch soon after Jesus' birth and he was still tetrarch at the time of Jesus' execution. Jesus' whole life is enclosed within Antipas's tetrarchy. While both the biblical and non-biblical sources inevitably portray Antipas from their own viewpoints, a reasonably complete and coherent picture of the tetrarch emerges. The net effect of a review of the various sources is that we are able to locate the ministry and movements of Jesus firmly within the historical context of Galilee at that time. Moreover, there are at least four intersection points between the two men, whether indirect or direct. Not only did Herod Antipas the tetrarch provide a context for Jesus' ministry in Galilee, but Jesus also proves to be rooted into that context.

Account of Jesus', *Bib* 66/3 (1985), pp. 344–363. Philo, *Legatio ad Gaium* 299–305, notes that Antipas was present in Jerusalem for Passover on another occasion, the incident of the gilded shields.

[76] Lk. 8:3.   [77] *Legatio ad Gaium* 299.

The high-priesthood of Annas and Caiaphas

Jerusalem was the domain of the high priest of the temple, who was also the president of the council of the Jews, the Sanhedrin. Since the annexation of Judea as a Roman province in AD 6, the high priest and the Sanhedrin had assumed new significance.[78] In the complex and technical religious society of Judea, Gentile Romans would be unwise to attempt to rule directly. The high priest, with senior associates called 'chief priests' (who appear to have been close family members),[79] formed a sacral oligarchy within the Sanhedrin. All power in Judea, and particularly in Jerusalem, was concentrated in their hands.[80] The high priest and the chief priests acted as surrogate to the Roman governor, answerable to him, governing the people in his place.

Since the annexation of Judea in AD 6 and throughout Augustus's remaining years until his death in AD 14, the high-priesthood had been dominated by one man, Annas. Tiberius's first prefect, Gratus, experimented with other high priests but soon returned to the Annas dynasty, appointing Caiaphas high priest in AD 18, a position he held until AD 37. Although Caiaphas fulfilled the office of high priest, it appears that he did so in the shadow of his father-in-law Annas. Annas's name continues to appear as high priest in the gospels and Acts even though he had technically relinquished that office nearly twenty years earlier.[81] Both men appear in the pages of Josephus, though it is from the New Testament that we discover the familial connection between them.[82] Caiaphas was son-in-law to Annas, a detail that explains how he came to be appointed in the first place and why Annas's name continued to appear as

---

[78] For the view that the Sanhedrin was a more *ad hoc* body, convened as need arose, rather than one with a standing authority over Jews outside Judea, see J. S. McLaren, *Power and Politics in Palestine: The Jews and the Governing of their Land 100 BC–AD 70*, JSOT Supplement Series 63 (Sheffield: JSOT, 1991), p. 97.

[79] See Acts 4:6. The *Lament of Abba Saul*, having listed the 'houses' of the high priests, adds, 'For they are the high priests; their sons are the treasurers of the sacred treasury of the temple, the Corban; their sons-in-law are temple officers' (Babylonian Talmud, *Pesahim* 57a).

[80] Did the high priest have jurisdiction in Idumea and Samaria, that is, in the non-Jewish part of the province of Judea? The existence of a council of the Samaritans suggests that these non-Jewish regions may also have had their own local governing bodies (*cf. Antiquities* xviii.87).

[81] See Lk. 3:2; Jn. 18:13, 24; Acts 4:6.   [82] Jn. 18:13.

79

high priest alongside his. In 1992 an ossuary (burial bone chest) was discovered in Jerusalem bearing the words 'Joseph son of Caiaphas'; Josephus refers to him as 'Joseph who is called Caiaphas' and 'Joseph surnamed Caiaphas'.[83]

Successive Roman emperors and their governors plainly felt that the Annas family served them well as surrogates. A perspective different from the Jewish viewpoint survives in the *Lament of Abba Saul*:

> Woe is me for the house of Hanin [= Annas].
> Woe is me because of their whisperings.

According to this *Lament*, the house of Annas was adept at political intrigue, at 'whisperings'. This is borne out in the gospels' account of their treatment of Jesus of Nazareth.

The synoptic gospels – Mark in particular – portray Jesus as aware that at his forthcoming visit to Jerusalem he would face rejection from the chief priests.[84] Clearly Jesus was not unaware that Jerusalem was their domain, at least in terms of worldly power and politics. The gospel of John notes that Jesus spent many weeks in Jerusalem in the period between the Feast of Tabernacles and the Passover.

His mounted entry into Jerusalem in a manner prophesied for Israel's king, his ejection of the merchants from the temple and his public teaching of the people in the temple precincts were deliberate actions challenging the authority of the temple hierarchy. Inevitably they confronted him with the question, 'By what authority are you doing these things, or who gave you this authority to do them?' Theirs came from the Roman emperor, mediated through his prefect. But who gave Jesus the right to act like this within their jurisdiction? Jesus gave his answer in the parable of the heir of the vineyard.[85] He was the last servant God would send to a people in rebellion, his 'beloved Son', whom, however, the 'tenants' would kill.

Even before his dramatic entry into Jerusalem in the weeks before Passover, the chief priests knew of Jesus. According to John's account, the Sanhedrin had already decided that Jesus must be arrested and put to death.[86] Their meeting with him in

---

[83] *Antiquities* xviii.35, 95.   [84] Mk. 8:31; 9:31; 10:32–34.

[85] The episode is recorded in Mk. 11:27 – 12:11.

[86] Jn. 11:45–53. An early tradition preserved in the Talmud confirms that a decision about Jesus was taken well ahead of the Passover:

the temple precincts during the week prior to Passover would have convinced them that here was a messianic claimant capable of securing a significant following, especially among the Galilean contingent now arriving for the Passover. Public order, for which they were responsible, was seriously jeopardized by this man. An outbreak of disorder would speak against the capacity of their family faction to hold office.[87] Jesus must be removed, and by stealth, before the crowds knew of it. Hence Jesus was arrested at night, interrogated throughout the night by the hierarchy in a series of meetings and brought to the prefect while most people in Jerusalem were asleep.

Whereas John the baptizer formed the context for the beginning of Jesus' ministry and Herod the tetrarch formed the context for his ministry in Galilee, the high priest and the Sanhedrin, with the Roman prefect, formed the context for his final days and hours in Jerusalem. The gospels establish Jesus' connection with this temple hierarchy. The gospel accounts of Jesus tie him into this historical landscape in Jerusalem.

The Roman trial and execution of Jesus

A Roman governor's working day began before dawn. By 9am[88] Jesus had been brought by the chief priests before the prefect, accused by them, condemned and crucified.

The prefect's trial of the accused was probably not the public affair it is commonly believed to have been, but conducted

---

Jesus was hanged on Passover Eve. Forty days previously the herald had cried, "He is being led out for stoning, because he has practised sorcery and led Israel astray and enticed them into apostasy. Whosoever has anything to say in his defence, let him come and declare it." As nothing was brought forward in his defence, he was hanged on Passover Eve (*Sanhedrin* 43a).

While there may be an apologetic motive here in establishing that due legal process was observed in relationship to Jesus, the passage in Jn. 11:45–53 appears to support some kind of proclamation against Jesus in the weeks prior to the Passover. According to the Johannine tradition, Jesus had been in and around Jerusalem in the months between the Feast of Tabernacles and the Passover. In other words, he was no absolute newcomer to Jerusalem, arriving from Galilee at the time of Passover.

[87] *Cf.* Mk. 14:1–2.

[88] Mk. 15:25 has 'the third hour', 9am, whereas Jn. 19:24 has 'the sixth hour', midday.

within the precincts of the military barracks.[89] The 'crowd' who demanded that Pilate should crucify Jesus were probably a group specially gathered by the chief priests, rather than the general populace of Jerusalem. As will be noted in the excursus following, Pilate was at that time significantly vulnerable to political blackmail. Despite Pilate's lack of conviction about Jesus' guilt for the crime of treason, Caiaphas the high priest and his associates had the upper hand. The governor bowed to their demands and so Jesus was led out to Golgotha for crucifixion as 'king of the Jews'. The crucifixion process was under way before most people in Jerusalem would have been aware of it.

Historically speaking, Jesus was killed because he was a threat to the chief priests' authority in Jerusalem and because a compromised governor was at that time able to be intimidated by them. Political expediency in the differing circumstances of the chief priests and of the Roman prefect led to the death of Jesus of Nazareth. The trial of Jesus fits in well with the circumstances suffered by Pilate after the fall, in AD 31, of Sejanus, his patron and protector, who had taken many steps against the Jews in Italy.[90] Subsequent to Sejanus's death, Tiberius wrote to his governors warning them against overturning Jewish customs. Pilate was quite vulnerable to Jewish blackmail and intimidation at the likely time of Jesus' arrest in AD 33. Once again, the gospel account fits well into a known context.

Conclusion

We have now reviewed five political and religious leaders, mentioned with others in Luke 3:1–2, who formed important parts of the historical context for the public ministry of Jesus of Nazareth. Too much should not be claimed for historical reconstructions of persons as distant from us as these men are. Those historical writers who individually or severally portray them have their own limitations and biases. Nevertheless, coherent and believable sketches of these men are possible, notwithstanding the limitations. The point is that these men, as

---

[89] That is, the Praetorium, Herod's former palace, now the prefect's headquarters in Jerusalem (*cf.* Mt. 27:27).

[90] Philo, *Legatio ad Gaium* 159–161.

mentioned with others by the historically minded Luke, enable us to establish a reasonably complete historical context and setting for the brief public ministry of Jesus of Nazareth. He is, indeed, a believable historical figure within the setting these men provide for him.

To be sure, our fullest picture of Jesus comes from the four gospels. Of that there can be no question. Nevertheless, each of his contemporaries, John the baptizer, Herod the tetrarch, Caiaphas and Annas the high priests, and Pilate the prefect, illuminates something of the social and political landscape in which Jesus was placed, and to that extent casts some light on him, or at least makes him more real, historically speaking. Not least, the historically based sketches of leading contemporaries offered in this chapter will help deliver Jesus from some of the more bizarre and idiosyncratic versions of him which continue to be presented.

Beyond that, however, it is clear that Jesus as presented in the gospels was in various ways connected with these people. He intersects with them. But the gospels' accounts of these intersections, for the most part, are given only in passing, enhancing their historicity. To be sure, once Jesus is in Jerusalem, the references to Jesus and the temple hierarchy and to Jesus and Pilate become expansive and pointed. In this regard, some have argued that the texts are apologetic – seeking, for example, to inculpate the Jews while exculpating the Romans. It is, however, quite legitimate to argue that the gospels have got both the high priest and Pilate right, and that Jesus was a victim of the political circumstances of the period after the fall of Sejanus, when Pilate would have been somewhat at the mercy of Jewish public opinion and negative dispatches back to Tiberius by the high priest. According to this view, which I regard as well founded and plausible, Jesus in the gospels can be seen to be historically tied back into that context. By way of analogy, Jesus and his historical context may be likened to a painting with Jesus in the foreground, and Herod Antipas, John the baptizer, Caiaphas, Annas and Pontius Pilate in the background. These five figures are not, however, merely background; they are also engaged with the one in the foreground, and at the same time with one another. It is a dynamic complex of relationships.

Excursus
The quest for the historical Pontius Pilate

For an otherwise obscure governor of a minor province with a small military command, Pontius Pilate is remarkably well attested in the ancient sources. In addition to the inscription bearing his name and title as 'prefect of Judea' discovered at Caesarea Maritima in 1961, he is referred to in the written sources by Tacitus, Philo, Josephus, the four gospels and the Acts of the Apostles. Yet he poses a major problem for the historian. The three main sources present him very differently. Philo's comments about Pilate are extremely hostile.[91] While Josephus is not so obviously biased as Philo, his descriptions of the governor are none the less quite negative. How then are we able to reconcile the ruthless figure of Philo (and of Josephus) with the vacillating one we encounter in the gospels? Naturally, the divergences have attracted the attention of scholars and several theories have been proposed to account for them. Two such views will be reviewed and a third proposed as the most likely approximation of the governor under whom Jesus suffered.

There is, first, the view that the picture of Pilate as the tough governor, as painted by Philo and Josephus, is more or less correct, and that the vacillating and ultimately accommodating Pilate of the gospels is a falsification. According to this reconstruction, which is chiefly associated with S. G. F. Brandon,[92] Jesus was in fact an anti-Roman insurrectionist (or an advocate of insurrection). Since the early church needed the good will of the Roman authorities, its founder's true sympathies must be masked. Hence the gospels present Jesus as innocent, a victim of Jewish machinations, with an indecisive governor portrayed as having been coerced into executing Jesus against his better moral judgment.

It is likely that the Romans were aware of and worried by the new sect from Judea. Though it was written half a century after the events described, the concern expressed in Tacitus's

---

[91] Whereas B. McGing, 'Pontius Pilate and the Sources', *CBQ* 53/3 (1991), pp. 416–438, holds a low view of Philo as a historical source, E. M. Smallwood, 'Philo and Josephus as Historians of the Same Event', in *Josephus, Judaism and Christianity*, ed. L. H. Feldman and G. Hata (Leiden: Brill, 1986), pp. 114–129, rates him higher than Josephus as to hard facts.

[92] *Jesus and the Zealots* (Manchester: Manchester University Press, 1967).

account of the spread of this 'superstition' to Rome and of its strength there in the 60s[93] would surely have been felt at the time. The gospel writers' sensitivity to this opinion may be reflected at a number of points. Mark significantly omits the assertion found in John that the Galilean crowd attempted to make Jesus 'king', even though Mark's account demands some detail of this kind to make sense of the flow of the narrative.[94] Luke's version of Jesus' trial by Pilate and his interrogation by Herod the tetrarch is careful to establish that Jesus did not engage in any treasonable kingship activities, whether in Galilee or Judea.[95]

Sensitivity to damaging opinion does not, of course, make that opinion true. The accusation of high treason brought to Pilate by the temple hierarchy, that he opposed payment of taxes to Caesar and claimed to be Christ, a king,[96] resonates remarkably with the crimes of a notorious Galilean who had in the not too distant past risen up against Roman rule in Judea. The uprising of Judas the Galilean, when Judea was annexed as a Rome province and direct personal tax to Rome was first levied, was doubtless well remembered by Roman officials in Rome. Judas was a rabbi, a Galilean and a populist[97] – a convenient and damaging stereotype to apply to Jesus, who was also a Galilean, a rabbi and a populist.

Roman military governors took seriously charges of this kind. One of their major responsibilities was to maintain peace and order within the provinces. The Roman military administration was quite severe in its treatment not only of leaders of movements, but also of associates and followers of those leaders who rose up against them. It must be assumed that Pilate carefully investigated these charges against Jesus and, had they proved true, would not only have executed him for treason (as indeed he did) but would also have acted severely against his followers. Had Jesus been the insurrectionist of Brandon's reconstruction, the Romans would have stamped out the Jesus movement then and there, as they had in the case of Judas's following.[98]

In short, the possible presence of some apologetic elements in

---

[93] See *Annals* xv.44.   [94] *Cf.* Jn. 6:15 with Mk. 6:45–46.
[95] Lk. 23:1–16.   [96] Lk. 23:2.
[97] See Josephus, *War* ii.118, 433; vii.253.   [98] Acts 5:37.

the gospels portraying Jesus as a non-revolutionary does not prove that he *was* a revolutionary, nor does it invalidate the essential integrity of the gospels in their presentation of Pilate as a rather indecisive figure at that time.

A second reconstruction proposes that the major sources are in fact in fundamental agreement, despite apparent divergences.[99] According to this line of argument, Pilate was a governor loyal to his emperor Tiberius, and his actions towards Jews and Samaritans, when compared to other governors, were relatively unremarkable. In fact, his ten-year incumbency was one of relative calm. His behaviour towards Jesus can be adequately accounted for by his ignorance of Jewish culture and politics along with a certain personal indecisiveness. There may have been just enough smoke, as it were, in the case of Jesus to justify extinguishing the fire. In any case, what importance, more or less, attached to one Jew? And did not the accused's stubborn silence in the face of interrogation amount to contempt of court (*contumacia*), something abhorrent to Romans?

While this reconstruction upholds the broad historicity of the gospels in the face of the Brandon alternative, it scarcely does justice to Philo's and Josephus's accounts of Pontius Pilate. Indeed, so far as we know, it was the provocative actions of Pilate after his arrival in Judea in AD 26 which broke the calm which had prevailed since Judas's rebellion twenty years earlier. In his brief chronological survey of Jewish history from the arrival of Pompey in 63 BC to the outbreak of the war with Rome in AD 66, Tacitus was to comment that *sub Tiberio ques*, 'under Tiberius all was quiet'.[100] This was to change during the next five years while the Praetorian prefect L. Aelius Sejanus was *de facto* ruler in Rome.

Pilate's introduction into Jerusalem of military standards bearing idolatrous icons was without precedent; previous governors had used unornamented standards. Similarly unprecedented was the issuing of coins bearing the offensive *lituus* and *simpulum* as used in Roman cultic practice. These actions cannot be explained away on the grounds of cultural innocence.

[99] See McGing, 'Pontius Pilate and the Sources', pp. 416–438.
[100] *Histories* v.9. See further P. W. Barnett, 'Under Tiberius All was Quiet', *NTS* 21 (1975), pp. 564–571.

They were calculated and deliberate. Indeed, in relationship with the iconic standards in Jerusalem, Josephus comments that 'Pilate . . . *decided* to overturn the laws of the Jews'.[101] Actions such as the seizure of money from the sacred treasury for the construction of an aqueduct in Jerusalem,[102] and the slaughter of the Galileans in the act of sacrificing the passover lambs,[103] are quite consistent with the provocatively introduced iconic standards and coins noted above.

Along with Barabbas, the two insurrectionists crucified with Jesus had participated in an otherwise unknown uprising against Roman rule.[104] Perhaps this disturbance was also provoked by Pilate's actions. The furore some time later over the gilded shields brought to Jerusalem, despite the absence of iconography, reflects the deep and justifiable suspicion of the people towards Pilate.[105] Aniconic these shields may have been, but the inscriptions dedicating them to Tiberius were almost certainly offensive.[106] Pilate's appointment in Judea effectively ended when he was dispatched to Rome to account for the slaughter of a number of Samaritans on Mount Gerizim.[107]

Josephus does nothing to qualify or downplay his report that the Samaritans complained that their people had gathered at Mount Gerizim 'not as rebels against the Romans', but as 'refugees from the persecution of Pilate'.[108] Josephus's description is but a milder and briefer version of Philo's portrayal of Pilate as 'naturally inflexible, a blend of self-will and relentlessness', who, according to Philo, 'feared exposure for his conduct as governor . . . the briberies, the insults, the robberies, the outrages and wanton injuries; executions without trial constantly repeated, the ceaseless and supremely grievous cruelty . . . his vindictiveness and furious temper'.[109] Even allowing for some rhetorical excess by Philo, the violence of the episodes recorded by Josephus, and Luke's brief but chilling reference to the slaughter of the Galileans, may well justify Philo's verdict.

---

[101] *Pilatos . . . epi katalysei tōn nomimōn tōn Ioudaikōn ephronēse* (*Antiquities* xviii.55).

[102] *Ibid.*, xviii.60–62.   [103] Lk. 13:1–2.   [104] Mk. 15:7.

[105] Philo, *Legatio ad Gaium* 299–305.

[106] See further P. S. Davies, 'The Meaning of Philo's Text about the Gilded Shields', *JTS* 37 (1986), pp. 109–114.

[107] Josephus, *Antiquities* xviii.85–89.

[108] *Ibid.*, xviii.88.   [109] *Legatio ad Gaium* 301–302.

But how can this Pilate be reconciled with the governor who comes before us in the gospels? A third reconstruction would indicate that both Philo and Josephus have portrayed Pilate correctly, but that at the trial of Jesus, due to changed political circumstances in Rome, Pilate had been forced to act out of character.[110] Thus each of the major sources can be viewed as historically consistent with the others. According to this line of thought, it is noted that Pilate's appointment to Judea more or less coincided with the beginning of Sejanus's appointment as Praetorian prefect. It will be remembered that Tiberius remained on the island of Capri during those years, leaving Sejanus as *de facto* ruler in Rome.

Philo, the Jew of Alexandria, states that Sejanus 'wished to make away with [our] nation', knowing that the Jewish people were loyal to Tiberius.[111] There is evidence that Sejanus, ambitious to grasp imperial power in Rome, harboured the desire for a ruler cult in honour of his deity.[112] This, too, would have contributed to an enmity against the Jews and their monotheistic beliefs. It appears to be no coincidence that Pilate 'decided to overturn the laws of the Jews' at the very time that the anti-Semitic Sejanus was at the height of his powers in Rome.

After the fall of Sejanus in October AD 31, however, Tiberius wrote to his provincial governors demanding that they 'speak comfortably to the members of our nation in the different cities . . . to disturb none of our established customs but even to regard them as a trust committed to their care . . .'[113] To no provincial governor would these words have been more appropriate than to the prefect of Judea, home of the Jewish people, even if we had no information about his actions. But we do. Josephus's descriptions of Pilate's behaviour, and Philo's verdict on Pilate, noted above, indicate the singular appropriateness of Tiberius's letter to his prefect in Judea, Pontius Pilate.

The incident of the gilded shields occurred in the post-

[110] The leading advocate of this reconstruction is P. L. Maier, 'Sejanus, Pilate and the Date of the Crucifixion', *CH* xxxvii (1968), pp. 3–13; 'The Episode of the Golden Roman Shields in Jerusalem', *HTR* lxii (1969), pp. 109–121.

[111] *In Flaccum* 1:1; *Legatio ad Gaium* 160. See E. M. Smallwood, 'Some Notes on the Jews under Tiberius', *Latomus* xv (1956), p. 325.

[112] Tacitus, *Annals* iii.72; iv.2, 72; Suetonius, *Tiberius* 48, 65; Dio Cassius lviii.2, 4, 5, 7.

[113] Philo, *Legatio ad Gaium* 160–161.

Sejanus situation.[114] Pilate is now accountable to a new master, the emperor Tiberius, who has forbidden further harassment of Jews. This will explain Pilate's speedy removal of the shields, upon the petition of the Herodian princes (including the tetrarch of Galilee-Perea, Herod Antipas). This he would not have done during Sejanus's incumbency. In the new situation, when Tiberius was again undisputed ruler, the Jewish temple hierarchy had the upper hand in regard to Pilate, especially in the light of his past behaviour towards the Jewish people. It is this 'new' situation that explains the 'new' Pilate as we encounter him in the gospels in his relationship to the Jewish leadership.

Under interrogation by the chief priests Jesus did not deny that he was the Messiah. This provoked the charge against him of blasphemy. But when they brought him to Pilate they converted the religious charge of blasphemy to one more recognizable and culpable to the Roman mind, the political charge of treason. Thus in each of the four gospels Pilate asks the political question of the accused, 'Are you the king of the Jews?'[115] Jesus' agreement with this charge would have been, in effect, a denial of Tiberius's kingship in Judea. Upon enquiry, however, Pilate decided that he must release Jesus. The charge of treason was not substantiated. But in the 'new' situation after the fall of Sejanus, the chief priests were able to intimidate the governor: 'If you release this man, you are not Caesar's friend; everyone who makes himself a king sets himself against Caesar.' They add, ominously, 'We have no king but Caesar'.[116] The man who had ridden roughshod over the Jewish people was now at the mercy of their leaders. And he knew it. One false move and his appointment would be cancelled and his career finished. And so Pilate acquiesced, handing Jesus over to the execution squad for crucifixion on the charge of treason, that he was 'the king of the Jews'.

[114] See further E. M. Smallwood, 'Philo and Josephus as Historians of the Same Event', pp. 126–128.
[115] Mk. 15:2; cf. 14:61. See Jn. 18:33.   [116] Jn. 19:12–16.

Chapter Five

Jesus in the gospels

Any reconstructed version of Jesus must explain the beliefs and practices of the early churches which were historically continuous with him. Before Easter, we have Jesus in company with his disciples. Immediately after Easter, we have the Jerusalem church founded by the same disciples. The Jesus who was followed before Easter was worshipped by those same people after Easter. In a short space of time there were other churches in Judea.[1] Such churches – in Jerusalem and Judea – are, historically speaking, early.

The continuity between the disciples before and after Easter does not depend on the narrative of Acts (which is problematic in the eyes of critical scholarship), but may be deduced from passing references in Paul's letters. Paul's letters support the assertion of Peter in Acts that 'God has made him Lord and Christ, *this* Jesus whom you crucified'.[2] The 'Christ of faith' is directly continuous with and therefore congruous with the 'Jesus of history'.[3] Yet, to generalize, neither the humanistic versions of Jesus of the nineteenth century nor the various versions of him in the latter decades of the twentieth century have done more than pay lip-service to the historical continuity between Jesus and these churches. Rather, the Jesus of these studies tends to be circumscribed within the context which has been created for him, whether social, religious or historical. Only elements of Jesus' humanity, and not his deity, are allowed to colour these studies. According to some, it is his Jewishness that is fundamental, whether as a charismatic Galilean rabbi (Vermes), an eschatological prophet (Sanders) or an oracular

---

[1] 1 Thes. 2:14; Gal. 1:22. [2] Acts 2:36; *cf.* 2:23, 32.

[3] This famous distinction was made in the late nineteenth century by M. Kähler, *The So-Called Historic Jesus and the Historic Biblical Christ* (Philadelphia: Fortress, 1964).

prophet (Horsley). Others see Jesus in Hellenistic terms, a figure resembling a wandering Cynic wisdom teacher (Crossan, Mack, Downing). Little attention is given to the 'deity dimension' in Jesus, belief in which is highly noticeable in the earliest churches. For this reason, these versions of Jesus resemble the 'pale Galilean' of nineteenth-century liberal Protestantism, against which Schweitzer reacted so vigorously.

There is little new in these nineteenth- and twentieth-century reconstructions. As early as the first century (some time after the Jewish war in AD 66–70) Jesus was regarded warmly by Mara bar Serapion as 'the wise king' whom the Jews executed but whom God avenged. The wise king did not remain dead but 'lived on in the teaching he had given'.[4] 'Wise king' though he was, this Jesus was not raised physically from the dead; only his teaching lived on. In the third century after Christ, Porphyry, an anti-Christian polemicist, wrote: 'Jesus is to be honoured as the wisest of men; he is not to be worshipped as God.[5] The veneration of Jesus as a man, while rejecting his deity, is thus no new thing.

If orthodox believers, in response, point to the exalted Christ preached in Acts as the continuation of the divine figure of the gospels, the rejoinder – typically – would be that Acts and the gospels merely portray the Christ of the later church's faith, and cannot be used without critical evaluation. My case, however, is based on the evidence of the Pauline letters. From these it can reasonably be argued that the gospels and Acts have got right the congruity of the Christ of the early church with the historical Jesus. As I have noted throughout, Paul's letters can be dated with confidence as literature close in time to Jesus, written by one who had been part of New Testament history almost from its inception, whether as persecutor or as apostle.

[4] F. F. Bruce, *Jesus and Christian Origins Outside the New Testament* (Grand Rapids: Eerdmans, 1974), pp. 30–31. Bruce thinks Mara bar Serapion was a non-Christian, a Gentile philosopher who bracketed Jesus with Socrates and Pythagoras as persecuted wise men who were each vindicated in different ways by God after their deaths.

[5] Quoted in R. Wilken, *The Christians as the Romans Saw Them* (New Haven: Yale University Press, 1984), p. 145.

The churches in Judea

In Paul's letters we find evidence of Christian churches in Judea in the time soon after Jesus. From 1 Thessalonians, written around AD 50, we learn of 'the churches of God in Christ Jesus' which suffered persecution in Judea from the Jews.[6] Can we establish a date for the existence of these churches? From the context it is likely that Paul is speaking of the existence of churches before 'the Jews . . . drove [Paul] out [of Judea]'. Paul was forced to leave Judea soon after his initial return as a Christian to Jerusalem, that is (by the best reckoning), c. AD 36/37.[7] It can be concluded that such persecuted churches were in existence by c. AD 36/37, that is, within four years of the first Easter.

We can, however, 'fix' the existence of churches in Judea even closer to Jesus. Paul told the Galatians that he 'persecuted the church of God violently and tried to destroy it'.[8] It is likely that Paul was converted within a year or so of the historical Jesus.[9] Thus the church which he persecuted, that is, the Jerusalem church, must have been in existence in the immediate aftermath of Jesus. Later in Galatians Paul speaks of other churches, 'the churches of Christ' in Judea.[10] After being forced out of Judea, Paul went back to his native Tarsus in Cilicia, where he preached 'the faith'.[11] There he heard of the reaction of 'the churches of Christ in Judea', namely, that they 'glorified God' because the persecutor was now preaching 'the faith he once tried to destroy'. These references in Galatians 1:13, 21–23 establish the existence both of 'the *church* of God' (in Jerusalem) which Paul persecuted in the time immediately after Jesus,[12] and of '*churches* of Christ' in Judea within three years or so of Paul's conversion, that is, within four years of Jesus. But there is reason to believe that they had come into existence earlier.

It is evident, too, that 'the faith', the body of belief that Paul

---

[6] 1 Thes. 2:14.   [7] Gal. 1:18, 21; *cf.* Acts 9:26–30.   [8] Gal. 1:13.

[9] M. Hengel, *Between Jesus and Paul* (London: SCM, 1983), pp. 30–31, gives AD 30 as the date of the crucifixion and AD 32–34 as the date of Paul's conversion. I suggest that AD 33 is preferred over AD 30 as the date of the crucifixion.

[10] Gal. 1:21, 23.   [11] Gal. 1:15–16, 18, 21–23; *cf.* Acts 9:30.

[12] 'The church of God' here refers to the Jerusalem church; *cf.* Acts 26:10.

the persecutor 'tried to destroy', must have been evil and dangerous in his eyes. The beliefs of the members of the Jerusalem church must have been blasphemous, and their behaviour schismatic, to provoke the wrath of the ultra-orthodox Saul of Tarsus.[13] What those beliefs might have been is hinted at by his comment that the churches of Christ in Judea 'glorified God' on account of 'the faith' Paul was now proclaiming in Cilicia, which he had previously attempted to destroy. The context of Galatians suggests that 'the faith' Paul was preaching in Cilicia and elsewhere was focused on an exalted view of the Son of God, whom Paul was now commissioned to proclaim to the Gentiles.[14]

This is information of remarkable historical importance. First, these are statements not made in a gospel or in Acts, but in a letter, written quite early in the ministry of the apostle Paul. Paul's references were made in passing and they were subject to checking and challenge; their historicity must be regarded as secure. Secondly, these texts establish the existence of the Jerusalem church from soon after the time of Jesus (and therefore in continuity with Jesus and those disciples who followed him during his ministry) and of other churches soon afterwards. Thirdly, this, our earliest window into the original churches, shows that they held an exalted view of Jesus; they were adherents of 'the faith' Paul had been trying to destroy. Fourthly, the exalted view of their Teacher, owing to his resurrection, nevertheless must have been consistent with his followers' view of him before the crucifixion. In other words, the resurrection must have made everything Jesus had said and done beforehand fall into place, as it were, so as to provide the ultimate explanation of his identity.

The implications of this for Jesus research are clear. Any

---

[13] Elsewhere Paul connects his persecution of the church of God out of zeal for the traditions of his fathers (Gal. 1:13–14) with 'righteousness under the law' (Phil. 3:6). Evidently Paul's attempt to 'destroy the faith' sprang from a perception that the churches in Judea had departed from those 'traditions'. There must also have been some connection between the Christological and the nomological (*cf.* M. Hengel, *The Pre-Christian Paul*, London: SCM, 1991, pp. 79ff.). Moreover, Paul appears to have regarded the crucified one as the 'accursed' of God since 'cursed is everyone who hangs on a tree' (Dt. 21:23; *cf.* Gal. 3:13). The persecutor Paul's 'knowledge' of Christ was, according to his own testimony, 'according to the flesh', superficial and misguided (2 Cor. 5:16).

[14] Gal. 1:16.

reconstructed view of the pre-Easter Jesus must be consistent and continuous with what the immediate post-Easter churches believed, and for which they were persecuted by Saul of Tarsus and other Jews. Any reconstructed version of Jesus must be historically suspect if it does not account for the persecution of his followers in the months following his execution. This was not the fate of inoffensive followers of benign prophets or devout rabbis. To be historically credible a reconstructed view of Jesus must be able to explain the early imprint of the exalted Jesus on the churches of Jerusalem and Judea.

From Jesus into the churches

Based on the letters, without reliance on the gospels or Acts, it is possible to gather an idea of the beliefs and practices of the first churches ('the faith') which, because of their historical proximity to Jesus, must owe their impetus and character to him. The examples of such beliefs which follow, based on the letters,[15] form a kind of 'Identikit' to which Jesus, as presented in the gospels, can be compared. The question is, can the portrayal of Jesus in the gospels be trusted?

In the first example, a word of Jesus may be heard in the earliest churches. It is the address of God as *abba*, 'Father'. This familial mode of speaking to God is almost unknown among Jews of the period.[16] The original Aramaic *abba* must have been so well known in Paul's congregations that he could use it, without explanation, in letters to Greek-speaking churches.[17] Most probably *abba* was transmitted by Jesus to the original disciples, who gave the word to Paul who, in turn, taught it to the Gentile churches. It may be significant in this regard that 1 Peter has the phrase, 'if you invoke as *Father* him who judges . . .'[18] The

[15] D. Wenham, *Paul: Follower of Jesus or Founder of Christianity?* (Grand Rapids: Eerdmans, 1995), has argued for the extensive dependence by Paul upon the details of the life and teaching of Jesus.

[16] J. Barr, 'Abba Isn't "Daddy"', *JTS* 39 (1988), pp. 28–47, argues that while *abba* was colloquial, it was not 'childish', or necessarily a reference to 'my father'. Nevertheless, Barr allows that *abba* as an address for God 'may have been first originated' by Jesus, though he questions how pervasive was its use by Jesus. J. D. Crossan, *The Historical Jesus: The Life of a Mediterranean Jewish Peasant* (San Francisco: Harper, 1991), pp. 146–147, has conveniently reproduced several possible parallels to Jesus' use of *abba*.

[17] Rom. 8:15; Gal. 4:6; *cf.* Mk. 14:36.   [18] 1 Pet. 1:17.

invocation of the Father in prayer, as reflected in the traditions of both Paul and Peter, points back to Jesus' distinctive teaching about God as Father.

Paul's letters reveal a remarkable redefinition of God. As a devout Pharisee, Paul would have repeated the synagogue benediction of 'the God of our fathers', whom he blessed daily, as 'One God'. Paul the Christian, however, writes of God as 'The God and *Father* of the Lord Jesus, he who is blessed for ever'.[19] Clearly the heart of Paul's understanding of God had undergone radical and dramatic change. What can account for this? Jesus' teaching of God as *abba* or Father, and Paul's conversion to Jesus the Lord, most plausibly explain this redefinition. Moreover, the God who is 'the God and Father of the Lord Jesus' is also 'our Father', the Father of his children, Christian believers.[20]

Closely connected, secondly, was Paul's preaching of Jesus as 'the Son of God',[21] in fulfilment of God's revelation 'in him' of 'his Son' near Damascus a mere year or so later than the first Easter.[22] Although there is no direct tradition in Paul tracing back his 'sonship' to the historical Jesus, it is clearly present in both the synoptic and the Johannine traditions.[23] At the least, the Pauline conviction of Jesus' 'sonship' coincides with the evidence of the gospels. But this filial, relational view of 'the Son of God' does not arise from either the Jewish or the Hellenistic religious culture.[24] In view of Jesus' use of *abba* or Father as a term of address for God, it is probable that it originated with Jesus.

Thirdly, the term 'kingdom' or 'kingdom of God' occurs frequently in the New Testament letters[25] yet it is rare in the Old Testament, and surprisingly seldom found in the Jewish writings[26] in the era of Jesus.[27] Since it is often used by Jesus,

---

[19] 2 Cor. 11:31.   [20] *E.g.* 1 Thes. 1:3.   [21] 2 Cor. 1:19; *cf.* 1 Thes. 1:10.

[22] Gal. 1:16.   [23] Mk. 13:32; *cf.* 12:16; Jn. 8:36; *cf.* Heb. 1:8.

[24] So M. Hengel, *The Son of God* (London: SCM, 1976), pp. 16–56.

[25] Rom. 14:17; 1 Cor. 4:20; 6:9–10; 15:24, 50; Gal. 5:21; Eph. 5:5; Col. 1:13; 4:11; 1 Thes. 2:12; 2 Thes. 1:5; 2 Tim. 4:1, 18; Heb. 1:8; 11:33; 12:28; Jas. 2:5; 2 Pet. 1:11; Rev. 1:6, 9; 5:10; 11:15; 12:10; 16:10; 17:12, 17–18.

[26] G. E. Ladd, *The Presence of the Future* (Grand Rapids: Eerdmans, 1974), pp. 130–133. Examples of the use of related terminology arc also rare in the Qumran literature: 'This shall be a time of salvation . . . an age of dominion for all the members of his company' (*War Rule* I); 'For thou art terrible, O God, in the glory of thy kingdom' (*War Rule* XII). Reference is made to the 'kingdom of his people' (*Liturgical Fragments* V).

[27] Nevertheless, it may be asked why this vocabulary was not even more

who included it in the Lord's Prayer, it most probably flows from Jesus' use into the letters.

A fourth observation may be made about the word 'Christ'. This word, which occurs hundreds of times in the letters of the New Testament, is quite rare in Paul's Bible, the Septuagint. Moreover, it is used there not in an absolute sense ('the Christ') but in a qualified sense ('the anointed of the Lord', or 'the anointed of God').[28] Paul did not derive his absolute use of the term 'the Christ' from his Bible.[29] While the word 'Christ' is chiefly used by Paul as a surname for Jesus,[30] it was initially a title,[31] as, for example, in Paul's references to 'Christ crucified' or to himself as 'an apostle of Christ Jesus', or as an 'ambassador for Christ'.[32] This service of the Christ did not begin with Paul; there were those (like Cephas and James) who were 'apostles [of Christ] before [him]',[33] that is, in the year or so between Jesus' death and Paul's apostolic call. Paul's use of the formal

frequent, for example, in Paul's letters, given its frequency on the lips of Jesus in the gospels. Was it because such a Semitic-sounding term would be less clearly understood by Paul's Gentile readers? Or, with greater probability, was it because Paul saw fit to express it rather differently from Jesus, being on the other side of the divide created by Jesus' death and resurrection? It has been plausibly argued that Jesus' 'kingdom' vocabulary before Easter becomes Paul's 'righteousness' vocabulary on the other side of Jesus' death and resurrection. A. J. M. Wedderburn, 'Paul and Jesus: The Problem of Continuity', *SJT* 38 (1985), pp. 202–209, explains the difference of vocabulary between Jesus and Paul as owing to Paul's experience of God's righteousness and Spirit within his own life.

[28] M. Hengel, *Studies in Early Christology* (Edinburgh: T. and T. Clark, 1995), pp. 1–2, points out that *christos* occurs only 37 times in the Septuagint.

[29] The hope of a 'messiah' arises out of OT hopes, especially after the exile (2 Sa. 7:8–16; Ps. 2:1–12; Is. 11:1; Mi. 5:1–3; Hg. 2:20–23; Zc. 9:9), but a prophecy of '*the* Messiah' is not found in precisely that terminology. Early Judaism looks forward to a messianic age, but there are few clear references to '*the* Messiah'. Rather, the term 'messiah' or 'anointed' is qualified, as 'anointed of the Lord', or 'his anointed' (*Psalms of Solomon* 17:32; 18:1, 5, 7). In apocalyptic thought, the specific figure is 'the Son of Man' (*2 Esdras* 13). See further F. Hahn, *EDNT* 3, pp. 479–481, with literature cited.

[30] Paul uses the word 'Christ' with remarkable frequency. It occurs more than 100 times in 1 and 2 Corinthians alone, letters written in the mid-50s.

[31] It is clear that, for the most part, Paul uses the word 'Christ' as a name, not as a title. Such a title would have been understood as 'he who had been smeared' (so Hengel, *Studies in Early Christology*, pp. 384–385), and would have been meaningless in the Gentile circles in which Paul moved, and to which he wrote.

[32] 1 Cor. 1:1; 2 Cor. 5:20; *cf.* Rom. 9:5.   [33] Gal. 1:17.

messianic title for Jesus must mean either that it derived from Jesus' own messianic consciousness or that the first Christians imposed that title on Jesus. The latter alternative raises the objection that the disciples are unlikely to have spoken of Jesus as 'the Christ' if this were not his own view of himself.

In this regard, Hengel has demonstrated that neither resurrection nor translation of righteous men to heaven established a notion of messiahship for those persons.[34] Jesus' messiahship cannot be explained – or explained away – by resort to the disciples' perceptions of a resurrected Jesus. Johannes Weiss saw the historical logic of this long ago when he asked, 'How could the belief in [Jesus'] messiahship emerge as a completely new phenomenon if he himself had not provided the impulse for it?'[35]

The belief, fifthly, that Christ 'died for' others is often stated within the New Testament.[36] From 1 Corinthians 15:1–5 we learn of a 'tradition'[37] which was 'received' by Paul – in all probability at the time of his conversion and baptism, from believers in Damascus[38] – which included the words, 'Christ died *for our* sins in accordance with the scriptures'. The scriptures in question

[34] Hengel, *Studies in Early Christology*, pp. 12–13.

[35] Quoted by Hengel, *ibid.*, p. 19.

[36] For example, 2 Cor. 5:21; Heb. 10:12; 1 Pet. 2:21; 1 Jn. 3:16, to take a sample across a number of NT writers.

[37] It is evident that the believers in the first churches 'received' and 'handed over' 'traditions' from Jesus. Paul states that he had received the tradition about the Last Supper 'from the Lord' (1 Cor. 11:23–25). Jesus' words and actions at the Last Supper have been 'received' by the original disciples, who in turn have 'handed over' these to Paul, who has in turn 'handed over' this 'tradition' to the Corinthians.

[38] Damascus at the time of Paul's conversion and call is a more likely occasion than at his first return visit to Jerusalem, from Cephas and James (*cf.* Gal. 1:18–19), for three reasons. First, such fundamental data must surely have come Paul's way earlier than three years from his conversion and call. What had he been preaching in and around Damascus? Secondly, a Damascus context would explain better the *en prōtois* of 1 Cor. 15:3: 'I delivered to you what I also received *at first*', that is, at his conversion and baptism. This makes at least as good sense as 'I delivered to you *as of first importance*'. Thirdly, a Damascus source of this tradition better suits the line of argument in Gal. 1:1–24, that Paul's message and his authority to proclaim it did not derive from the Jerusalem apostles (1:1, 12, 16–17, 19, 22). Nevertheless, the 'tradition' quoted in 1 Cor. 15:1–5 would have emanated originally from the Jerusalem apostles prior to being found in Damascus.

appear to be Isaiah 52:13 – 53:12, where the Servant of the Lord is put to death 'for . . . sins',[39] that is, the sins of the people. Because he is quoting a received tradition, it means that this scripture has been significantly reshaped by someone earlier than Paul.[40] Someone has changed Isaiah's prepositions, 'concerning sins' (*peri hamartias*) and 'on account of sins' (*dia tas hamartias*)[41] to 'on behalf of sins' (*hyper tōn hamartiōn*). A vicarious sense has been superimposed upon Isaiah's text by changes of preposition. But who changed it: disciples between Paul and Jesus, or Jesus himself? It is noted that Mark and Luke follow separate traditions for the Last Supper. Yet *hyper*, 'on behalf of', appears in both Mark's and Luke's accounts.[42] Both traditions articulate the *hyper*-concept. The idea that Jesus' death was 'on behalf of others', so frequently found across the New Testament letters and in the underlying gospel traditions, most probably goes back to Jesus himself, at the Last Supper, and quite possibly also on other occasions.[43]

Sixthly, it is evident that the churches addressed in the letters were expected to be praying communities,[44] and that the writers were steeped in prayerfulness. 'Pray for us' is their repeated request.[45] The benedictions, or blessings of God, found in the letters have echoes of the formal benedictions of the synagogue liturgies, now Christianized, implying a degree of parallel formality in the churches. The many other references to prayer and thanksgiving in the letters, however, speak of free and spontaneous supplication, implying, in all probability, a greater freedom in praying than was expressed within the Jewish synagogues of the period.[46]

Prayerfulness, liturgical and extempore, in the early churches

---

[39] Is. 53:12.

[40] A non-Pauline use, which may support a pre-Pauline use and therefore a pre-Pauline origin of *hyper* related to the death of Christ, is found in 1 Pet. 2:21–24, a passage which also echoes the same Servant Song (Is. 53:4, 5, 6, 12).

[41] Is. 53:10, 12.   [42] Lk. 22:19–20; 1 Cor. 11:24; Mk. 14:24.

[43] For example, Mk. 10:45, on which see P. Head, 'The Self-Offering and Death of Christ as a Sacrifice in the Gospels and the Acts of the Apostles', in *Sacrifice in the Bible*, ed. R. T. Beckwith and M. J. Selman (Carlisle: Paternoster, 1995), pp. 112–114.

[44] *E.g.* Jas. 5:13; 1 Pet. 4:7; Rev. 8:4.

[45] *E.g.* 1 Thes. 5:25; 2 Thes. 3:1; 2 Cor. 1:11; Rom. 15:30; Col. 4:3; Heb. 13:18.

[46] This is not to imply that Jewish prayer at the time was fixed immovably. At

and by the leaders and letter-writers most probably did not just begin *de novo*, or evolve over a period. It is far more likely to have been in continuity with the Teacher, who was noted in the gospels for his life of prayer:[47] something that appears to have deeply influenced the original disciples, and through them the believing communities in Judea and beyond.

In relation to this, it is striking (seventhly) that the early Christians also prayed *to* Jesus, now exalted. An example of such prayer is the brief Aramaic invocation *Maran atha*, 'Our Lord, come!' embedded in 1 Corinthians 16:22, which appears to have arisen originally in the worship of the Aramaic-speaking churches in Judea. A Greek version of this invocation appears also in Revelation 22:20, 'Amen. Come, Lord Jesus!' Jesus had taught the disciples to pray for God's kingdom to come. In the light of Jesus' ministry and resurrection, however, it is evident that God's kingdom will be manifested at Christ's return; hence the reshaped prayer, 'Our Lord, come!' or 'Come, Lord Jesus!' which is a prayer of the post-resurrection church. On view here in this brief prayer are both the example of Jesus' prayerfulness continuing in the early churches, and also his exalted status, with invocations directed *to* him.

As a final example, there is reflected in the letters a pattern of citing texts from the Jewish Scriptures. Prominent among these citations are the words from Psalm 110:1, 'The LORD said to my Lord, Sit at my right hand . . .' It is likely that these words underlie the early church's *Maran atha*, 'Our Lord, come!' as well as the many references in the letters to Jesus 'the Lord',[48] who is at God's 'right hand'.[49] The use of such texts is common within the letters. Did the letter-writers themselves begin to find

---

Qumran new prayers and hymns appear to have been composed. In mainstream Judaism R. Abbahu is said to have spoken 'a new benediction every day' (Babylonian Talmud, *ber* 4.8a). For reference to *ad hoc* synagogue prayers see S. C. Reif, *Judaism and Hebrew Prayer* (Cambridge: Cambridge University Press, 1993), pp. 99–100.

[47] See M. Bockmuehl, *This Jesus: Martyr, Messiah, Lord* (Edinburgh: T. and T. Clark, 1994), pp. 125–144.

[48] See 1 Thes. 1:1, 6; 2:15, 19 for randomly chosen references to Jesus as 'Lord' in an early letter.

[49] See *e.g.* Rom. 8:34; Eph. 1:20; Col. 3:1; Heb. 1:3; 1 Pet. 3:22. For discussion on the significance of Psalm 110 in the formation of early Christological understanding see Hengel, *Studies in Early Christology*, pp. 119–225.

in Jesus a fulfilment of their Scriptures, or was this something which had been begun, before Easter, by Jesus himself? In my view, there is no good reason to doubt that Jesus referred to this fulfilment theme, including Psalm 110:1,[50] and that his exegesis of this and other texts came to influence the way the first Christians thought about him.[51]

More could be written. But enough has been said to demonstrate that Jesus' resurrection, and also his anterior ministry as Teacher, gave the impetus for the formulation of traditions which would inform the churches and be broadened into various theological statements. Jesus' approach to God as *abba* also carried on into the churches, including those in Galatia and Rome which were geographically remote from Palestine. Moreover, Jesus' kingdom preaching to Israel is echoed across the letters of the New Testament. The tradition that Jesus was 'the Christ' and that his death was vicarious ('for others'), which is to be found in the apostolic writings, almost certainly stemmed from Jesus himself. His extensive prayerfulness is amply re-expressed and enjoined as an example within the letters of the New Testament. And the prayer addressed by him to *abba* ('May your kingdom come') becomes a prayer addressed *to* him, *Maran atha,* 'Our Lord, come!' Significant, too, is the apostles' recognition that texts like Psalm 110:1 were now fulfilled in Jesus' resurrection and ascension as Lord, at God's right hand. Here is a pattern of fulfilment-exegesis which most probably derives from Jesus himself.

The scattered data from the letters of Paul serve to establish a grid by which a profile of Jesus can be established. This is somewhat filled out by information about Jesus found, in particular, in 2 Corinthians, which gives a sweep of his birth, personal manner, nature of ministry, crucifixion and resurrection.[52] This profile is incomplete. How could it be otherwise? The letters do not set out to be biographical in regard to Jesus. But from these sources we catch a glimpse of one whom we see in much greater detail in the gospels. We see enough in the

---

[50] See Mk. 12:25–30; *cf.* Acts 2:36. Hengel, *Studies in Early Christology*, p. 173, does not think it is impossible that this text played a role in the teaching of Jesus, but it is not easily proved. R. T. France, *Jesus and the Old Testament* (London: Tyndale, 1971), p. 102, points to Mk. 14:62 as proof that Jesus did in fact apply this psalm to himself.

[51] *Cf.* Jn. 2:22; 12:16.   [52] See above, pp. 47–50.

letters to encourage us to believe that the gospels have got Jesus right. Someone fitting the portrayals in the gospels left the imprint we find in the letters of Paul and the other letters of the New Testament.

The problem of the Jesus of tradition for the reconstructed versions of Jesus

The point of my argument is this: historical reconstructions of Jesus must attribute to *him* – his person and his resurrection – the percussive impact which establishes the momentum and the trajectory of early Christianity, its worship and 'the faith' its apostles preached. This trajectory and momentum are evident in the letters of the New Testament and confirmed by the Acts of the Apostles. As M. Bockmuehl puts it, 'It is historically legitimate to see Jesus of Nazareth in organic, causal continuity with the faith of the early church.'[53]

We should go further. Not only is such a 'causal continuity' between Jesus and the faith of the early church 'historically legitimate', but any lesser interpretation would be historically implausible. Congruity dependent on continuity – a 'knock-on' effect between Jesus and the post-Easter church – is the most plausible explanation for the phenomenon of the existence, worship and preaching of earliest Christianity. The Jesus of Nazareth who ministered in Galilee, then to Gentiles to the north and east, and finally came to Jerusalem where he was crucified, is the same Jesus – 'this Jesus'[54] – who was immediately exalted in the church of Jerusalem and in the churches of Judea. But the current reconstructed versions of Jesus portray him as anything but this, whether some kind of prophet, sage or gnomist. None of these versions of Jesus is a Jesus who continues on into the life and faith of the early churches.

---

[53] Bockmuehl, *This Jesus*, p. 8. *Cf.* B. F. Meyer, *The Aims of Jesus* (London: SCM, 1979), 'it is . . . in the traditions generated by Jesus that we discover what made him operate in the way he did' (p. 252). See also B. Witherington, *The Christology of Jesus* (Minneapolis: Fortress, 1990), pp. 1–2, and quotations from de Jonge and Hurtado.

[54] Acts 2:36.

Problems in reconstructing Jesus from the gospels

Are we able to get back to the historical Jesus from the canonical gospels? Can we reconstruct an account of Jesus based on the gospels? What part is played by background studies in the search for the Jesus of history? Can we get back to Jesus by these studies? Here we face several problems.

One is that Mark and John set Jesus in different geographical backgrounds. Mark chiefly narrates Jesus as a preacher and teacher in Galilee, with a ministry also to the north and the east of Galilee; he comes to Jerusalem only once, at the end. John, however, devotes most space to Jesus in Jerusalem, in public dispute with the Pharisees and in private ministry to his disciples. So different are their contents that it is difficult to combine Mark and John.[55]

A second problem is that each of the four gospels is complete in itself. Each is a discrete literary entity, whose integrity and unity would be destroyed if they were merely amalgamated with the others. The gospels are analogous to four portraits of Jesus. On one side, painting their subject, are three French impressionists, Monet, Renoir and Pissarro. Renoir and Pissarro (representing Matthew and Luke) have their easels behind Monet (representing Mark) and they are influenced to a degree by his portrait. On the other side, not influenced by them and not influencing them, is van Gogh (representing John). As we inspect the four paintings we find that they do have the same subject, Jesus. Yet they remain four separate and idiosyncratic portraits which we cannot combine, consolidate or reduce to one presentation.

The third and major problem is that of a biographer's or historian's subjectivity.[56] Jesus represents a special obstacle to objectivity. For most people, believers and unbelievers, Jesus is an ideal figure, a hero, the embodiment of good. Human ideals, however, are variable, depending on one's personal temperament, worldview, and expectation of the perfectibility or otherwise of persons and society. Jesus readily becomes the

---

[55] See excursus, pp. 111–114.

[56] On the problem of the subjectivity of the interpreter see Bochmuehl, *This Jesus*, pp. 2–7.

objectification of such ideas and hopes – for example, as the liberator from structural, social or sexist oppression. When either text-based or holistic techniques are applied to Jesus studies, it seems that subjectivism comes into effect, so that we all tend to pick and choose what we wish from the range of data in the gospels. Even if there is a noble determination to embrace all the evidence, as indeed there should be, that evidence is probably subconsciously graded and classified, and given uneven weight.[57]

We have four discrete *bioi* or biographies[58] of Jesus; a fifth is not possible.

A counsel of despair?

This, however, is not a counsel of historical despair. While we may not rewrite the four gospels as a fifth, we are able to establish the historicity of a number of incidents in the gospels by a process of cross-checking. Here the gospel of Mark is helpful in assessing the historicity of John on the one hand, and Matthew and Luke on the other.

Careful comparison of the texts of Mark and John indicate that neither of these gospels is dependent on the other. Yet they have a number of incidents in common: for example, the feeding of the five thousand,[59] the anointing of Jesus,[60] Jesus' mounted entry to Jerusalem,[61] the arrest of Jesus,[62] Peter's denial of Jesus,[63] Jesus' trial before Pilate,[64] the soldiers' mockery

---

[57] If this is true for those who inhabit the world of 'un-faith', it is true also for those who belong to the household of faith. Despite all good efforts, we are left with the overall impression of eclecticism and subjectivity in the admirable attempt at historical reconstruction of Jesus' inner persona in Witherington, *The Christology of Jesus*. Cf. Kähler, *The So-Called Historical Jesus*, p. 111, who referred to the 'shifting sands of scholarly opinion'.

[58] See my discussion of the gospels as *bioi*, biographies, of Jesus, below, pp. 152–158.

[59] Jn. 6:1–14; Mk. 6:30–44 and pars.

[60] Jn. 12:1–8; Mk. 14:3–9 and pars.

[61] Jn. 12:12–19; Mk. 11:1–10 and pars.

[62] Jn. 18:1–11; Mk. 14:42–50 and pars.

[63] Jn. 18:15–18; Mk. 14:66–72.

[64] Jn. 18:28–40; Mk. 15:1–15 and pars.

and torture of Jesus,[65] the crucifixion at Golgotha,[66] and the burial of Jesus in the tomb of Joseph of Arimathea.[67] The vocabulary used in these incidents is quite different, yet the details are in such agreement that Mark and John are evidently describing the same events. Clearly each of the finished gospels arises out of different tradition streams, thus indicating multiple independent witnesses to a significant range of events in the ministry of Jesus.[68]

The feeding of the five thousand is a good example.[69] Close study of the texts of Mark and John shows that neither writer has looked over the other's shoulder. There is scarcely any vocabulary in common between the two. Moreover, the setting of the two accounts is different; Mark's is a climax to the mission of the twelve, while John's arises out of the multitude's desire to see more miracles at Jesus' hands. The two accounts are plainly the final versions of earlier and quite separate traditions, whether oral or written. Thus we have two witnesses to the one event. Whatever their differences and nuances, each points to that great occasion at springtime when Jesus fed five thousand men with their families seated on green grass with five loaves and two fishes, leaving twelve baskets of surplus food.

Mark's account is also helpful as a template by which to measure the accuracy of Matthew and Luke. It is broadly agreed that both Matthew and Luke had access to a version of Mark, whether the text known to us or an earlier version. It is possible to assess what Matthew and Luke do with Mark's text: whether, for example, they make Jesus more exalted than Mark's original does. Does Matthew or Luke make a God out of the man they found in Mark? In fact they do not; their work proves them to be

[65] Jn. 19:1–4; Mk. 15:16–20 and pars.

[66] Jn. 19:17–24; Mk. 15:21–32.

[67] Jn. 19:38–42; Mk. 15:42–47.

[68] This was classically argued by P. Gardner-Smith, *Saint John and the Synoptic Gospels* (Cambridge: Cambridge University Press, 1938). For a comprehensive survey of the relationship between John and the synoptics see R. Kysar, 'The Contribution of D. Moody-Smith to Johannine Scholarship', in *Exploring the Gospel of John*, ed. R. A. Culpepper and C. C. Black (Louisville: Westminster John Knox, 1996), pp. 3–8.

[69] See P. W. Barnett, 'The Feeding of the Multitude in Mark 6/John 6', in *Gospel Perspectives* 6, ed. D. Wenham and C. Blomberg (Sheffield: JSOT, 1986), pp. 273–293.

sober and restrained writers.[70] These painters may have been influenced by Mark's portrait, but they have not romanticized his picture, though they have their own perspectives on Jesus.

Thus, comparative studies of Mark and John establish them as discrete literary works resting on earlier but separate traditions, bearing witness to Jesus. Close study of Matthew and Luke alongside Mark points up the integrity and competence of Matthew and Luke. We are able to approach the gospels as serious and responsible biographical works which yield helpful information about Jesus. We are able to relate to him through the gospel accounts without violating our own sense of probity.

A historical account of Jesus

Within limited terms, some historical details of Jesus can be determined in several areas. Although many scholars reject the attempt to do so, the duration and broad outline of Jesus' public ministry can be established. Based on Mark's account of Jesus' ministry in Galilee and surrounding regions, and on the occurrence of the feasts in John, it is likely that Jesus' ministry was not more than four years in length and not less than three.[71]

Jesus' public ministry throughout that period of three to four years may be roughly sketched as follows. Although his baptism by John was a critical moment bringing Jesus out of obscurity into the public arena, it appears that he remained in John's shadow until the baptizer's arrest. Then, however, Jesus' ministry, which was concentrated in Galilee, attracted more people and from further afield than did John's ministry, which was confined to the Jordan. Jesus also visited Jerusalem for the great feasts, where he engaged in dispute with the Pharisees. At first Jesus was able to teach in the synagogues of Galilee, but his teaching proved to be unacceptable to the Pharisees, so that the door to the synagogues was soon closed to him. He now preached in the fields and by the lakeside. He chose and trained twelve disciples, whom he sent to the towns of Galilee, announcing the coming of the kingdom of God and casting

---

[70] So P. W. Barnett, *Is the New Testament History?* (London: Hodder and Stoughton, 1984), pp. 99–110.

[71] See excursus, pp. 111–114.

out demons in his name. As a climax to their mission to Galilee, a great crowd gathered and attempted to make him king (messiah). As a result he was forced to withdraw from Antipas's jurisdiction for ministry in adjacent Gentile regions. Finally, he set out for Jerusalem, where, at the Passover, he was interrogated by the temple authorities and handed over to the Roman governor, who executed him for treason against Rome.

Moreover, we can gain, to some degree, an impression of Jesus as he would have appeared to his contemporaries. There is no reason why the gospels' frankness about Jesus' divisiveness should be doubted. These details are rather negative and possibly damaging to the presentation of him in the gospels. His own family declared him to be mad,[72] and the religious teachers regarded him as demon-possessed,[73] a false teacher and a blasphemer.[74] These latter views are consistent with the traditions about Jesus recorded in the Talmud, that he was a false teacher who led Israel astray, and who was hanged on the eve of Passover.[75]

But this does not appear to have been the verdict of the common people of Galilee. Jesus had been baptized by John and, like John, proclaimed a message about the kingdom of God.[76] John was revered as a prophet, and in all probability Jesus, too, was regarded as a prophet.[77] In his prophetic forecast of the imminent intervention of God's rule it appears that he portrayed himself as the Son of man, that is, as the divine agent of the kingdom of God spoken of by Daniel. While he was pointing obliquely to himself in this regard, it is by no means clear that his contemporaries understood this.[78]

Various scholars have seen Jesus as a prophet of some kind. In my view they may have erred in attempting to say too precisely what kind.[79] But they are probably correct in identifying him, at least in his public persona, as a prophet.

---

[72] Mk. 3:21; cf. Jn. 10:20.   [73] Mk. 3:22; Jn. 10:20.
[74] Mk. 2:6; Jn. 9:16; 10:33.   [75] Sanhedrin 43a.
[76] Mk. 1:14–15; cf. Mt. 3:2.   [77] Jn. 6:14; Mk. 6:14–15; 8:28.
[78] See C. Caragounis, The Son of Man (Tübingen: Mohr, 1986), pp. 247–250, for discussion as to what extent Jesus himself was a 'parable' to his contemporaries.
[79] R. A. Horsley and J. S. Hanson, Bandits, Prophets and Messiahs (Minneapolis: Winston, 1985), pp. 135–189.

But Jesus would have conformed to another role, that of a teacher or rabbi.[80] As noted above, Jesus taught in synagogues;[81] there is no good reason to doubt this. He was both referred to and addressed as 'teacher' and 'rabbi',[82] by those of his own circle and by others;[83] again there is no need to cast doubt on this. Josephus's description of him as a 'wise man' suggests the idea of a rabbi.[84] That the local Galilean as well as the Jerusalem scribes disputed with him is indirect evidence that he was a rabbi, if somewhat heterodox. (Rabbis did not debate with the populace, but with their peers.) His initiative in gathering an inner group of followers, who were his daily companions, and whom he taught and instructed at greater length, is consistent with his appearance as a rabbi or teacher. Indeed, it is possible that the house at Capernaum became, under Jesus, a kind of Galilean rabbinic academy or *haburot*, an alternative to the rabbinic houses in Jerusalem.

If his role as prophet at large was, as it were, his public face, then his role as a rabbi or teacher became his private face, known mostly to the immediate circle of followers.[85] There are many hints that Jesus explained his public teaching to them in private.[86] Things which the crowds did not understand he would unravel for them, including the parables, which were to the unreceptive crowds an instrument of divine punishment.[87]

It was as a rabbi that Jesus established his traditions with his

[80] See M. Wilcox, 'Jesus in the Light of his Jewish Environment', *ANRW* ii (1982), pp. 131–195.

[81] Mk. 1:21, 39; Lk. 4:16–21.

[82] The term 'rabbi' (literally, 'my master') was used rather loosely at the time of Jesus. After the war with Rome in AD 66–70, 'rabbi' came to be used in a more formal way of an ordained teacher. See E. Schürer, *The History of the Jewish People in the Age of Jesus Christ* II (Edinburgh: T. and T. Clark, rev. edn. 1979), pp. 325–326.

[83] The roles of prophet and rabbi may not have been mutually exclusive. Individuals who belonged to the mass who regarded him as a prophet also addressed him as rabbi or teacher (Mk. 10:17; Jn. 9:1).

[84] *Antiquities* xvii.63. It is noteworthy that Josephus had applied his term 'wise man' for Jesus previously to Solomon and Daniel (*Antiquities* viii.53; x.237). See further B. Witherington, *The Jesus Quest* (Downers Grove: IVP, 1995), p. 162.

[85] See P. W. Barnett, *The Two Faces of Jesus* (London: Hodder and Stoughton, 1990).

[86] See *e.g.* Mk. 4:10–20; 7:17–23; 9:28–29; 10:10; 11:20–25.

[87] See Mk. 4:10–12, 33–34.

circle of disciples, using various methods of rhyme, aphorism and parable. They came to him, took his yoke upon them and learned from him.[88] The 'tradition' which would be 'delivered' to the churches and which would ultimately find its way into the gospels had its origin in the traditions Jesus 'handed over' to the disciples and which they 'received'. It was in this intimacy of the rabbi with his disciples that Jesus taught them to know God as he did, as *abba*, and to pray to God as their *abba*, and in what terms (as in the Lord's Prayer). It will have been in such private settings, too, that Jesus taught them on the way to Jerusalem, as well as in Jerusalem, about humility, serving one another, the coming of the Spirit, his own future return, and (at the Last Meal) the tradition about remembering him on into the future in the breaking of the loaf and the sharing of the cup.

The public face, that of the prophet, was forgotten by the people at large soon enough, impressive though he had been. So, too, was John the baptizer soon forgotten, though he, too, had been impressive.[89] A number of Jewish prophets were to have their supporters in the coming decades, but their followers quickly dispersed upon the deaths of their leaders.[90] It was otherwise with Jesus. The private face by which Jesus revealed his inner relationship with God, the fact and meaning of his death and the coming of the Spirit, together with patterns of discipleship, were etched deep in the minds of his close companions. In turn, these disciples would 'deliver' the teaching of Jesus to others.

But not even this teacher–disciple intimacy would account for the existence of exalted beliefs about Jesus evident in the church in Jerusalem and the churches of Judea. Had Jesus' death been the end, even his 'sheer originality'[91] would not have

---

[88] *Cf.* Mt. 11:28–30, where Jesus' invitation is cast in rabbinic terms. Hengel, *Studies in Early Christology*, pp. 73–117, argues that Jesus was the Spirit-anointed teacher of the wisdom of God.

[89] It is noted, however, that the Nabatean invasion of Antipas's region in the mid-to-late 30s was seen as a divine punishment for the tetrarch's treatment of John the baptizer almost ten years earlier (*Antiquities* xviii.116–119). He was not forgotten immediately.

[90] For references and discussion see P. W. Barnett, 'The Jewish Sign Prophets – AD 40–70: Their Intentions and Origin', *NTS* 27 (1980–81), pp. 279–297.

[91] The striking phrase used by C. F. D. Moule, *The Origin of Christology* (Cambridge: Cambridge University Press, 1978), p. 8.

brought the churches into existence. If his person with them was the firewood, it was his resurrection from the dead and the Spirit he sent which lit the fire that would soon blaze across the world. And it was his resurrection,[92] together with the coming of the Spirit to the first believers, in particular the apostles, which caused his words and works first to be 'remembered'[93] and then to be written in the texts we call the New Testament.

The gospels, history and faith

What is the relationship between the Jesus of various historical reconstructions, including the one offered here, and faith? Is faith directed towards such a figure? The mere asking of the question creates a sense of unease. Given that there are so many reconstructions, we ask, 'Whose reconstruction should we choose and why?' Is faith only for the historically informed and the historically inclined, who have the technical ability to verify the accounts?

According to the New Testament, faith responds to the gospel, the word of God, spoken and written. Paul would answer, 'Faith comes by hearing and hearing from the word of Christ.'[94] Here faith is the response of the ear to the spoken word. John would answer, 'These [signs] are written [in this book] that you may believe that Jesus is the Christ.'[95] Faith, then, is a response to the word of God; it is not a response to history, or to historical reconstructions *per se*. Moreover, it is the claim of the New Testament and the reality of experience that the gospel is self-authenticating. This comes by the activity of the Holy Spirit.[96]

What purposes, then, are served by the historical enquiry to which this book, in part, is devoted? First, it is necessary from time to time to provide some defence of the intellectual and historical credibility of the gospel record which is the object of faith. People need to have confidence in the gospel they are called upon to believe. Secondly, it is important to understand that Jesus is a genuine figure of history. The incarnation, the atonement and the resurrection are not merely redemptive ideas; they involved a real man at a specific time and place. The

---

[92] See excursus, pp. 128–131.   [93] See Jn. 2:22; 12:16; 14:26.
[94] Rom. 10:17, my translation.   [95] Jn. 20:30–31.
[96] 1 Cor. 12:2–3; Gal. 4:6.

gospel is not gnostic, which it would be apart from Jesus' true rootedness in history. A gnostic gospel is an obligation-free gospel; Jesus would be one lord among many. By contrast, according to the Christian gospel, his uniqueness and the claims of his lordship arise out of his historical particularity.

Faith which saves is faith in Christ. This faith comes by reading about him in the canonical gospels and by hearing about him in the preached gospel. But this Jesus is a genuine figure of history whose similarity to the one we meet in the canonical gospels can be demonstrated by the logic of history, by identifying the earliest churches' faith, which we are able to do by a careful analysis of the letters of Paul, in particular. Such analysis shows that the gospels have got Jesus right; we have not been misled by them. We can place our trust in Christ with moral confidence. Our own integrity is not violated in doing so.

Excursus
Overview of Jesus' ministry[97]

The difficulties of establishing a 'history' of Jesus' ministry are well known. First, there appear to be fundamental differences between John's apparent theological approach and the synoptics' apparent historical approach. How can such seemingly different styles of gospel-writing about Jeus be combined so as to form one narrative? Traditionally, scholars have not regarded John as valuable for historical reconstructions of Jesus, seeing it at best as supplying only supporting evidence.[98]

Secondly, such historical data as there are in John are difficult to reconcile with the data in the synoptics. In the synoptics, apart from the nativity story in Luke, Jesus visited Jerusalem only once, at the Passover at which he was executed, whereas John portrays Jesus at Jerusalem feasts early in his ministry, in chapters 2 and 5. Further, according to John 7 – 11, Jesus was in and around Jerusalem for the six months prior to his death, that is, between the feasts of Tabernacles and Passover. But in what must have been roughly the same period, Mark 7 – 9

[97] See H. Hoehner in *DJG*, pp. 118–122.
[98] For the view (with which I am in qualified agreement) that the synoptic gospels should be made to fit in with John's sequence, see J. A. T. Robinson, *The Priority of John* (London: SCM, 1985), pp. 1–36.

locates Jesus making his way from the Gentile territories to the north of Galilee through Galilee and Perea to Jerusalem.

The view that the synoptics are historical and John is theological must, however, be qualified. It is now apparent that in their own ways the synoptics are also 'theological', and that their geographical-historical references can serve a 'deeper' meaning. Mark, followed by Luke, invests the narrative about Jesus with a profound sense of purpose. Thus as soon as John the baptizer is imprisoned Jesus' ministry begins; the one follows the other, back to back, as it were. With greater historical probability, however, John portrays Jesus working for a period *in parallel* with the baptizer, in his shadow until the imprisonment.

This note of high purpose is also to be seen in Mark's and Luke's use of Jesus' *one* journey to Jerusalem as a motif for a disciple's sacrificial 'following' of Jesus. This is not to deny the historical truth of that journey, but merely to observe that the writers' theological intentions appear to have given a deliberate shape to the narrative. Their emphasis on purposive discipleship based on Jesus' final journey would explain why the synoptics Mark and Luke only describe one journey to Jerusalem.

John, unlike the synoptics, sees Jerusalem, not Galilee, as Jesus' 'own country' where he had no honour.[99] Hence in John we find Jesus more often in Jerusalem than in Galilee, more often in conflict (that is, not honoured) in Jerusalem than in Galilee. Again, this is not to deny historical truth to John's account, but to observe that his theological perspectives have determined where his details are concentrated, that is, in Jerusalem.

John's perception of Jerusalem as Jesus' epicentre, and his interest in the disputes there at the great feasts, may assist the historian with an overall chronological framework of Jesus' ministry. The feasts help us calculate the length of Jesus' ministry. On this basis Jesus' ministry began before the Passover visit to Jerusalem in chapter 2, and extended over at least two subsequent years, punctuated by the Passovers of chapters 6 and 12.

By contrast, Mark's perception that Nazareth in Galilee was Jesus' 'own country' where he was not honoured means that he

[99] Mk. 6:4; *cf.* Jn. 4:43.

has concentrated his account in the general Galilee area. While chronological details are more vague in Mark, they are not altogether missing. The plucking of grain in Mark 2:23 indicates one spring or summer, and the 'green grass' of 6:39 ('much grass', Jn. 6:10) points to a subsequent spring, following the mission of the twelve to the towns of Galilee. Thus, counting backwards from the Passover or spring when he was executed, the gospel of Mark points to a ministry period of at least two years.

Thus we employ John for Jesus' and the baptizer's over-lapping ministries, for an overall feast-based chronology of Jesus' history, and for events in Jerusalem. For his part, Mark narrates Jesus' activities in Galilee and adjoining regions. By using John and Mark (in particular) we are able to build up a broad picture of Jesus' ministry, even if there are parts of the landscape which remain incomplete.

The possibility of overall reconcilability of John and Mark is supported by the congruence between them *in the same sequence* of five critical reference points:

	John	*Mark*
1. John's baptism of Jesus	1:32–33	1:9–11
2. Imprisonment of John;	3:24	
beginning of Jesus' ministry in Galilee	4:3, 43, 47	1:14–15
3. Jesus feeds the five thousand	6:1–15	6:30–45
4. Jesus leaves Galilee for Judea	7:9–10	10:1
5. Jesus' final arrival in Jerusalem	12:1	11:11

Helpful though John is in establishing overall chronology and sequence as punctuated by the feasts in Jerusalem, there is a problem in regarding Jesus' ministry as of only about two years' duration. The three Passovers in John require a two-year period, plus however many months Jesus worked in parallel with John the baptizer before the first Passover. But it is difficult to squeeze Jesus' ministry in Galilee, his call and training of the twelve and their mission to the towns of Galilee into the one year between John's first and second Passovers. I therefore propose that, for whatever reason, John has omitted to mention an intervening Passover between the first and second Passovers. Perhaps the unidentified 'feast of the Jews' of 5:1 was, in fact, a Passover.

The boundaries of Jesus' ministry are marked by the ministry of John the baptizer which began in AD 28, and Jesus' execution at Passover AD 33. On this basis I suggest the following chronology for Jesus' ministry:

Year

28	The appearance of John the baptizer	
29/30	Ministry in parallel with John the baptizer	
		Passover: John 2 – 3
31	Imprisonment of John the baptizer Ministry in Galilee	
		[Passover: John 5:1?]
32	Ministry in Galilee	
		Passover: John 6
	Gentile territories Jerusalem and Judea	
33	Arrest, trial, execution	Passover: John 12

Chapter Six

Jesus and the spread of early Christianity

The death of Jesus (in AD 33, in my view) is a fixed point, historically speaking. Between Jesus and the written gospels there took place a process of collecting the underlying sources and forming them into finished products. This process apparently occurred over at least several decades. During this period of gospel preparation, Christianity was not hidden from our view, though it is often assumed that this was the case. In fact, we know a great deal about the history of early Christianity. A helpful sketch can be established from the letters of Paul. These are datable and close in time to Jesus, and provide gratuitous historical information about Jesus and also the apostolic age. In terms of the process of historical enquiry, they provide an important alternative to the Acts of the Apostles, which is an edited version of various unknown sources, whose date of authorship and intended readership are not certainly known.[1]

As we have seen from evidence in Paul, it is clear that the movement was in existence in the immediate aftermath of Jesus. Equally, it can be shown that it spread rapidly in the following years. By the mid-50s, as Paul reveals in one letter, he had proclaimed the gospel in an arc from Jerusalem to the borders of Illyricum (the former Yugoslavia).[2] From the direct evidence of his letters, we know of his pioneer ministry in the kingdom of

---

[1] This is not to imply the unreliability of Acts, or, for that matter, the entire objectivity of the letters of Paul. The early chapters of Galatians, for example, are not 'straight' biography, but use biographical information to put a case for Paul's independence of authority from the leaders of the Jerusalem church. In regard to the historical character and reliability or otherwise of Acts, see M. Hengel, *Acts and the History of Earliest Christianity* (London: SCM, 1979), p. 61; C. J. Hemer, *The Book of Acts in the Setting of Hellenistic History* (Tübingen: Mohr, 1989), pp. 159–220; B. W. Winter (series editor), *The Book of Acts in its First-Century Setting*, 6 vols. (Grand Rapids: Eerdmans, 1993–).

[2] Rom. 15:19.

Arabia (Nabatea) and in the Roman provinces of Cilicia, Galatia, Macedonia, Achaia and Asia.[3] Also from his letters we know, by inference, of the ministry of others which resulted in the formation of churches in Jerusalem, in wider Judea, in Damascus, in Antioch and in Rome itself. Acts proves to be corroborated to a remarkable degree by the letters, but at the same time it fills out and elucidates the briefer picture found in the letters. The two sets of documents illuminate each other so as to give an impressive sweep of the history of the early church.

It is clear that this period should not be considered a mythic or 'holy' era of unreal 'stained-glass figures'; it is recognizably historical. One indication of this is that this history at many points dovetails with known elements of secular history.

AD 33–47 according to Galatians 1:3 – 2:8

The first two chapters of Paul's letter to the Galatians provide a series of windows through which we can catch glimpses of the unfolding history of the first years of the apostolic age, the period between the death of Jesus and the climax of the New Testament era in the writing of the gospels and Acts. First, in the aftermath of Jesus we see a church – the church in Jerusalem – under severe persecution by Paul (c. AD 33/34).[4] Secondly, within three years of his Damascus road encounter with Christ (in c. AD 34), we see Paul, now a believer, back in Jerusalem in the house of Cephas/Peter and also meeting another apostle, James, the brother of Jesus (c. AD 36).[5] Thirdly, soon afterwards, when Paul is in Cilicia we see the churches (plural) of Judea glorifying God (c. AD 36/37), having heard that the former persecutor is now proclaiming the faith he had previously tried to destroy.[6] Fourthly, within fourteen years of the Damascus road Christophany (i.e. c. AD 47), we see Paul again in Jerusalem, now conferring with the 'pillars' of the church in Jerusalem: James, Cephas and John.[7]

This fourth window, the meeting in Jerusalem in about AD 47, is a particularly interesting viewing-point. Through it may be observed, fleetingly as it were, the fourteen or so years of the history of the apostolic age going back to Jesus, in which there

---

[3] Gal. 1:17/2 Cor. 11:32–33; Gal. 1:22–23; 1:2; 1 Thes. 1:1; 1 Cor. 1:1; Col. 1:1.
[4] Gal. 1:13.   [5] Gal. 1:15–19.   [6] Gal. 1:21–24.   [7] Gal. 2:1–10.

had been two apostolates,[8] or missions: one to Jews, the other to Gentiles. Cephas had been entrusted with the gospel to the circumcised, while Paul – hitherto unrecognized by the Jerusalem leadership – had been entrusted with the gospel to the Gentiles.

Paul the founder of Christianity?

Was Paul the founder of Christianity, or at least the catalyst for a radical redirection of the movement? Many scholars as well as lay people hold that Paul had just that role. The early chapters of Galatians, however, will not allow these views. As the pre-Christian Saul, he had attempted to destroy 'the church of God' and 'the faith' which were already in existence.[9] He speaks of those who 'were apostles before' him,[10] and of whom, in Jerusalem, he now comes to enquire.[11] Although Paul argues throughout these chapters for the independence from others of his apostolic call, none the less we are in no doubt as to the existence and prior authority of those in Jerusalem who were leaders before him. It is the Jerusalem 'pillars', James, Cephas and John, who recognize Paul's ministry and who agree that he should go to the uncircumcised and they to the circumcised.[12] This is all from their side. It is a unilateral, not a multilateral, agreement. The existence and authority of various leaders before Paul, to whom he must defer, is quite clear from Galatians 1 – 2, as well as from the pen of Paul's apologist Luke in the account of the uncontested leadership of James at the Jerusalem Council in about AD 49.[13]

The prominence of Paul's letters in the New Testament and the space and importance devoted to him in Acts by Luke must not blind us to the existence and activity of other missions and their leaders. Had the Jews not rejected the message of Jesus the Messiah, these other missions, which were directed to the Jews, may have assumed a greater historical prominence. The evolution of Christianity as a Gentile movement by the 60s inevitably enhances Paul's role from later perspectives. At the time, however, powerful figure though he was, Paul was but one among others in the missionary endeavour.

---

[8] *Apostolē*, Gal. 2:8.   [9] Gal. 1:13, 23.   [10] Gal. 1:17.
[11] Gal. 1:18–19.   [12] Gal. 2:7–9.   [13] Acts 15:13–21.

AD 33–47 according to the Acts of the Apostles

Acts fills out this picture. Peter, with John, evangelized Jerusalem and witnessed an ingathering of Hellenists, that is, Greek-speaking Jews.[14] Saul's persecution fell chiefly on them, scattering them away from Jerusalem. One of their number, Philip, evangelized the Samaritans, then the Hellenistic seaboard towns from Azotus in the south to Caesarea in the north of Judea, and probably beyond to the Graeco-Phoenician ports of Ptolemais, Tyre and Sidon.[15] Unnamed Hellenists took the gospel further up the eastern Mediterranean coast, eventually establishing the church in Antioch, capital of Syria.[16] Meanwhile, Peter was active outside Jerusalem, in Samaria and Caesarea, confirming Philip's ministry among Samaritans and Godfearers, but also among people in Judea,[17] and in all probability in Galilee as well.[18] For his part, Paul too had been active, first in Arabia, based in Damascus, and then, after a brief visit to Jerusalem, in his native Cilicia, including Tarsus.[19]

Thus throughout this earliest phase of apostolic history, almost from the beginning, there were two apostolates, Peter's among Jews, and Paul's among Gentiles. The Hellenists – Philip, and unnamed ones – had played a critical role. But they were not a recognized apostolate, that is, a mission led by an apostle. Philip, who was known as 'the evangelist', settled in Caesarea. Unlike Paul and Peter, he appears not to have become an itinerant missioner, except in the general area of Caesarea.

AD 33–47: the broader stream of history

The genuinely historical character of early Christianity emerges when it is placed in the context of the broader stream of 'secular' history. It is significant how often people and events within the biblical documents can be identified within that history.

Relationships between the new movement and the broader stream of history in AD 33–47 were influenced by the identity

---

[14] So M. Hengel, *Between Jesus and Paul* (London, SCM, 1983), pp. 1–29.
[15] Acts 8:4–40 *passim; cf.* Acts 15:3; 21:3–6, 7; 27:3.
[16] Acts 11:19–21.   [17] Acts 8:24–25; 9:32 – 11:18 *passim.*   [18] See p. 151.
[19] Acts 9:31.

and policies of the succeeding emperors, Tiberius (AD 14–37), Caligula (AD 37–41) and Claudius (AD 41–54).

Events during the principate of Claudius provide the best examples. We learn from Josephus that in AD 41 the new emperor, Claudius, appointed Agrippa as king of Judea, not only to repay his boyhood friend's assistance in securing his appointment as emperor, but also to bring stability to his Jewish subjects after the turmoil created by Caligula. In Agrippa's favour was his descent from the line of the Maccabees, illustrious forebears who had heroically delivered the Jews from the Greeks and, moreover, purified the temple from its desecration under Antiochus Epiphanes. Despite his profligate character and underlying Gentile sympathies, Agrippa succeeded in making the Jews believe that he was a devout and observant Jew. Josephus notes that Agrippa 'enjoyed residing at Jerusalem and he did so constantly and he scrupulously observed the traditions of his people. He neglected no rite of purification, and no day passed for him without the prescribed sacrifice.'[20]

Consistent with this, Agrippa assumed the role of champion of Jewish religious nationalism. He interceded with Claudius over Jewish rights in Alexandria, fortified the walls of Jerusalem and sought to convene a meeting of Jewish client kings of the region, perhaps in some kind of mutual defensive league.[21] Agrippa's assault on the leaders of the Jerusalem church, reported in Acts, appears to have been part of the policy of winning Jewish support for his rule. His execution of James Zebedee (possibly in place of his brother John) was followed by his arrest of Peter during the feast of the Passover, almost certainly with the intention of killing him, too.[22] For Peter, with John Zebedee, had baptized Samaritans; he had also eaten with the Gentile Cornelius and baptized members of his household.[23] It appears that King Agrippa regarded his attack on the leaders of the Jerusalem church as important. Only when all his efforts against them had failed did he leave Jerusalem to take up permanent residence in Caesarea.[24] Revealing his truer Gentile sympathies there, Agrippa publicly presented himself to the

[20] *Antiquities* xix.331.
[21] The latter actions tended to sour relationships with his patron, Claudius.
[22] See Acts 12:1–5. [23] Acts 8:14–25; 10:1 – 11:18. [24] *Cf.* Acts 12:19.

people of Caesarea as a Hellenistic god-king, only to be publicly struck down in the act of doing so, to the fierce pleasure of both Josephus and the author of Acts, who independently record the event.[25]

Though a friend of Agrippa, Claudius did not prove to be a supporter of Jews at large within the empire. Upon assuming office in AD 41, his declared policy towards the Jews in Alexandria was quite severe, promising dire punishment in the event of further local disturbances.[26] In the same year he forbade Jews to assemble in Rome.[27] In AD 49 he actually expelled the Jewish population from Rome, a detail mentioned in Acts.[28] Jews everywhere, including those within Judea, would have felt that the protection they had enjoyed under Augustus and Tiberius was now considerably weakened. Paul, the Jew, was apparently not able to visit Rome on account of Claudius's policies.[29] Only after the emperor's death did he make plans to visit there.[30]

It was also at this time ('in the days of Claudius'),[31] that is, in the mid-40s, that Agabus, a Christian prophet, with other prophets from Jerusalem, visited the multi-ethnic church in Antioch, prophesying a widespread famine in that region. Some time later the believers in Antioch sent relief to the elders of the church of Jerusalem by the hands of their leaders, Barnabas and Saul.[32] The famine added to the woes of the post-Agrippa era. The rise of banditry caused by famine was quickly followed by banditry of a more political kind. In about AD 47, Jacob and Simon, the sons of the dynastic warlord Judas the Galilean (who was killed in the uprising over the poll-tax census in AD 6), arose in rebellion, only to be captured and crucified.[33]

These points of intersection between early Christianity and 'secular' history establish that the history of early Christianity is, indeed, genuinely historical and not 'mythical' in character.

---

[25] *Antiquities* xix.344–349; Acts 12:21–23.
[26] 'Claudius' Letter to the Alexandrians' 90–100, in C. K. Barrett, *New Testament Background: Selected Documents* (New York: Harper and Row, 1961), p. 46.
[27] Dio Cassius lx.6.
[28] Suetonius, *Claudius* xxv.4; Acts 18:2. See above, p. 31.
[29] Rom. 1:10, 13, 15; 15:23.   [30] *Cf.* Acts 19:21.   [31] Acts 11:28.
[32] Acts 11:29–30.   [33] *Antiquities* xx.102.

Galatians 2:9–10: looking to future ministry

The meeting of leaders in Jerusalem in about AD 47 was important for the direction of their future missions. Unfortunately Paul does not say what transpired after it was agreed that he (with Barnabas) should go to the Gentiles, while James, Cephas and John should go to the Jews. Notwithstanding the lack of further information, this passage, more than any other in the New Testament, explains the subsequent history of the apostolic age.

The reader is immediately struck by the formal confirmation by the Jerusalem 'pillars' of the apostolate of Barnabas and Paul to the Gentiles. Less obvious, but equally important, is the fact of an ongoing apostolate to the circumcised, led by James, Cephas and John. This was not an agreement between equals. Clearly the Jerusalem leaders enjoyed some kind of primacy, for it was they who agreed that Barnabas and Paul should go to the Gentiles while they, for their part, should go to the Jews.[34]

This year (c. AD 47) marks the beginning of two recognized apostolates, one to Jews, the other to Gentiles. The passage of time, however, was to witness significant changes to this straightforward arrangement. Within a few years Peter and John had moved from Judea, though probably still ministering to Jews. Then, it appears, their ministry target widened to include Gentiles. By the time the literature of their missions was completed, it seems that Peter and John were directing their labours exclusively towards Gentiles. In time the two missions recognized in Jerusalem in about AD 47 had divided into four missionary groups.[35]

The mission group we know most about is Paul's. He is the

---

[34] Likewise the Jerusalem Council of AD 49 was not a meeting of equals who reached a democratic decision. Peter, Barnabas and Paul each spoke, but James declared what was to happen (Acts 15:6–21). The apostles and elders of the Jerusalem church sent their own delegates with Paul and Barnabas to Antioch, and it was they who explained the letter from the council (Acts 15:22–34). Clearly the Jerusalem church enjoyed a primacy in relationship with the church of Antioch.

[35] This is not to suggest there were no other mission activities. We know of Barnabas's journey to Cyprus with John Mark (Acts 15:39) and, less certainly by later hints, of Andrew's journey to Russia and Thomas's to India (see J. Foster, *After the Apostles*, London: SCM, 1961, pp. 22–28).

focal figure of the Acts of the Apostles, dominating its narrative from chapter 13 onwards. More particularly, we have Paul's own letters, which tell the story of his apostleship from the inside, as it were. The combined information about Paul from Acts and from his letters makes him one of the best-documented persons in antiquity. We are able to trace the history of his mission, and understand the difficulties he faced, over a period of thirty or so years from about AD 34 to about AD 65.

The mission to the circumcised is less straightforward. From Acts we know that James remained in Jerusalem and continued not only as a leader but, in the absence of Cephas and John, as the sole leader of the church of Jerusalem until his martyrdom in AD 62. It is almost certain that James, as brother of the Lord, was also the symbolic leader of the churches of Judea and Galilee.

In the years AD 33–47, mission work and persecution took Cephas/Peter in and out of Jerusalem. The details of his movements in the early years of his apostolate to the Jews in Samaria and Judea (and possibly Galilee) are known only from Acts. His later movements are known only by scattered references in Paul's letters, 1 Peter and the post-apostolic writer, Clement of Rome. By the late 40s we are able to trace Peter's movements to Antioch, and perhaps beyond Syria into the provinces of Asia Minor. Next he appears in Corinth some time later than AD 52, when Paul's first visit to Corinth ended.[36] It appears that Peter was following the same basic route Paul had taken earlier. Presumably his mission was to reach the Jews in those regions. Some time after his sojourn in Corinth, Peter reached Rome, perhaps by the mid-50s. It would appear that he remained in Rome until his martyrdom under Nero in about AD 65.

John's movements are even less certain. By the 50s his name disappears from records of activity in Judea. Only the book of Revelation, written from Patmos to churches in Roman Asia, uses the name 'John' (as author) in literature written after the meeting in Jerusalem in about AD 47.[37] Apart from patristic information, for any idea of his circumstances beyond the late 40s we are dependent upon the traditional ascriptions to John of the fourth gospel and of his three letters. Patristic sources locate

[36] 1 Cor. 1:12; 9:5.   [37] Rev. 1:1.

122

him in Ephesus, the great city of Asia.[38] This does cross-check with the 'John' of Revelation, who is so well known that his name alone is sufficient to call for the obedience of the churches of Asia.

The turmoil in Judea and the great Judaizing[39] controversy[40]

The 50s were dominated by the great controversy between Paul and those Jewish Christians who sought to impose the tenets of Judaism upon Gentile converts. This dispute appears to have been fuelled by the political turmoil in Judea as the people moved closer to the outbreak of open hostilities with Rome. Although the dispute dominates a number of Paul's letters and forms a significant part of the historical backdrop to the era when the gospels came to be written, the gospels give little or no echo of this debate. This is the more striking since the various traditions about Jesus would have been formed and gathered throughout these years.

Turmoil in Judea

The formal recognition of an apostolate to Gentiles in Jerusalem in about AD 47 occurred at a time when Jews in Judea were profoundly unsettled. The death of a popular Jewish king, Agrippa 1, in AD 44, was followed by the return of the Roman legions. Matters were to deteriorate further. In Rome, Claudius expelled the Jews from the city (AD 49).[41] In Judea,[42] under the procurator Cumanus (AD 49–52), Jewish religious scruples were to be repeatedly violated. A soldier blasphemously exposed his private parts in the temple precincts during Passover. Another publicly tore up a scroll of the Torah. Galileans were killed by Samaritans, with no Roman reprisals.

[38] 'John the disciple of the Lord, who also reclined on his breast, issued a gospel while living at Ephesus in Asia' (Irenaeus, *Against the Heresies* III.i.1; *cf.* II.xxii.5; III.iii.4).

[39] Strictly, the term 'Judaize' means 'live as a Jew' rather than 'impose Judaism on non-Jews' (see Gal. 2:14).

[40] For suggestions about the impact of contemporary circumstances in Judea upon the Judaizing mission against Paul see P. W. Barnett, 'Opposition in Corinth', *JSNT* 22 (1984), pp. 3–17.

[41] Suetonius, *Claudius* xxv.4.   [42] See Josephus, *War* ii.223–245.

Under the procurator Felix (AD 52–60) affairs in Judea were to deteriorate to an unprecedented degree.[43] Felix came to power in the twilight of Claudius's principate and continued throughout the early years of the young and inexperienced Nero. A former slave, Felix had actually married the young Jewish princess Drusilla, something deeply offensive to Jews. There are hints that Felix harboured aspirations to royalty. Tacitus comments that 'Felix played the tyrant with the spirit of a slave'.[44]

Felix's procuratorship was marked by a harsh campaign against the banditry which had flourished in consequence of the protracted famine. Josephus states that 'of the brigands whom [Felix] crucified, and of the common people who were convicted of complicity with them and punished by him, the number was incalculable'.[45] Even allowing for some overstatement, we are left with a grim picture. Tacitus notes that Felix 'plunged into all manner of cruelty and lust'.[46] The problem of Felix's incumbency was compounded by the character of the notoriously corrupt high priest Ananias, who held office from AD 48 to 59, and who seized sacrifices from the temple for his own use.[47]

Josephus mentions three movements which arose in Felix's time and which he appears to connect with the governor's extreme policies. First, he describes the rise of the *Sicarii* faction,[48] whose *modus operandi* was to murder noted Jews known to be sympathetic to Roman interests.

Secondly, Josephus writes of 'sign prophets' at that time: 'Under the pretence of divine inspiration fostering revolutionary changes, they persuaded the multitude to act like madmen, and led them out into the desert under the belief that there, God would give them signs of liberation.'[49] Josephus does not say what these promised 'signs' were. Given that the locale was the

---

[43] *Ibid.*, ii.246–270. [44] *Histories* v.9; cf. *Annals* xii.2. [45] *War* ii.253.

[46] *Histories* v.9. Allowance must be made for the tendency of Josephus to blame evil governors for the problems in Judea and for Tacitus's bias against people of non-senatorial background. Nevertheless, Felix emerges badly from the sources.

[47] Babylonian Talmud, *Pesahim* 57a.

[48] So named after the Latin curved dagger which they concealed under their flowing garments (*War* ii.254).

[49] *War* ii.259.

desert – so evocative in the salvation history of Israel – it is likely that the signs were expected to include those performed by Moses and Joshua at the time of the exodus and conquest. The 'liberation' would have been a re-enacted defeat, in the manner of Joshua, of the enemies of the moment, the Roman occupying force.

Thirdly, Josephus refers to some kind of an alliance between these apocalyptic prophets and various brigands in actions of a political, but religiously inspired, nature. In a frenzied manner these organized themselves in companies threatening to kill any who submitted to Roman rule. They moved through the countryside murdering those who supported Rome, setting fire to many houses.[50]

Such was the world of Judea after AD 47 when the apostle Paul began his missionary journeys to Galatia, Macedonia, Achaia and Asia, establishing congregations of predominantly Gentile composition.

Paul's apostolate to the Gentiles and the Judaizing reaction

Upon Paul's return to Antioch at the end of his first journey (to the uplands of central Anatolia), a serious dispute arose between him and Cephas/Peter, caused by the arrival from Jerusalem of 'certain men from James'.[51] At about that time[52] Paul heard that troubles over Judaizing had arisen in his newly established Galatian churches.[53] The Galatian churches were troubled by a man who led a group of Jews[54] who urged that circumcision was a prerequisite for membership in the Israel of God.[55] These agitators and their leader were putting pressure on other Jewish believers to force Gentile members to be circumcised.[56]

The Jerusalem Council met soon afterwards (c. AD 49) to resolve the question of Gentile observation of Jewish practices. The believers from among the Pharisees advocated circumcision and full observance of the law of Moses.[57] Significantly, the Pharisees were involved, whether actively or passively, in the

---

[50] *Ibid.*, ii.264–265.   [51] Gal. 2:11–14; Acts 15:1–2.
[52] The dating and provenance of the letter to the Galatians are debated.
[53] *Cf.* Acts 15:23–24.   [54] Gal. 5:10, 12; 3:1; 1:7, 9.
[55] Gal. 3:6–14; 6:16.   [56] Gal. 6:12.   [57] Acts 15:5.

struggles and crises of the period between Jews and Romans.[58] The religious zeal of the more nationalistic Pharisees cannot but have flowed over into questions raised by Paul's mission to the Gentiles. The times in which mission work among Gentiles began in earnest, therefore, coincided with difficult years in Judea.

It was from this environment of intensifying problems under Felix and Ananias that a group of missioners set out for Corinth in the mid-50s with the deliberate objective of overturning Paul's influence in the church in Corinth. To them Paul's mission to the Gentiles would easily have appeared to betray the cause of Israel.[59] They sought to re-impose some kind of Torah observance and righteousness upon the Corinthians.[60] For his part, Paul devoted extensive parts of 2 Corinthians to responding to their accusations against him.[61]

No problem in early Christianity surpassed that of the troubled relationship between Judean Christianity, which was culturally part of the rising tide of religious nationalism in Palestine in the 40s and 50s, and Paul's apostolate among the uncircumcised. The issue underlies many of Paul's letters, including Galatians, Colossians, 2 Corinthians, Romans, Philippians and 1 Timothy.

The truth of the gospel

On two occasions in particular, one in Jerusalem and the other in Antioch, there were bitter disputes over what Paul termed 'the truth of the gospel'.

First,[62] Paul returned to Jerusalem fourteen years after his great watershed call *en route* to Damascus. He was concerned to confirm the acceptability to James, Cephas and John of the gospel which he preached among the Gentiles, a gospel which did not require circumcision of Gentiles. Paul brought with him, as a test case, the uncircumcised Titus. While Paul's apostolic authority was independent of Jerusalem, it was important that his circumcision-free Gentile converts were accepted, along with believing Jews, as spiritual heirs of Abraham. It needed to be established that despite the decision to approve two apostolates,

---

[58] A Pharisee, Saddok, had collaborated with Judas the Galilean in the uprising against the Romans in AD 6. The 'Fourth Philosophy' had an underlying Pharisaic outlook. See Josephus, *Antiquities* xviii.1–10.

[59] Acts 21:20–21.   [60] 2 Cor. 3:3, 7–9; 11:15, 22.

[61] 2 Cor. 2:17 – 4:6; 10:12 – 12:12.   [62] Gal. 2:1–10.

based on Jewish and Gentile distinctiveness, there was over-arching agreement in the fundamentals of the gospel based on the death and resurrection of Christ.[63] The result was that Paul's view of 'the truth of the gospel'[64] was not challenged.

Secondly,[65] when Cephas had come from Jerusalem to Antioch he had shared table fellowship (perhaps including the Lord's Supper) with Gentile members. Though a Jew, Peter now lived 'like a Gentile'; that is, he had eaten with Gentiles, which meant eating what they ate, free of customary Jewish scruples. But when 'certain men came from James',[66] whom Paul calls 'the circumcision party', Cephas 'drew back and separated himself' (from eating with the Gentile members of the church). Paul 'opposed' Cephas 'to the face, because he stood condemned' for withdrawing into an exclusively Jewish table fellowship. It was hypocritical for Peter to 'live like a Gentile' but now by this action to 'compel the Gentiles to live like Jews'. At stake in Antioch was 'the truth of the gospel', threatened by the demand that the Jewish Christians must eat separately from Gentile believers.

The 50s were years of great difficulty as Paul established congregations among the Gentiles at a time of deteriorating circumstances in Judea. At opposite poles were Paul and the Judaizing missioners who sought to capture his churches for their brand of Jewish messianism. Remarkably, the dispute about 'the truth of the gospel' does not appear to have left an imprint on the gospel traditions then being formed, nor in the finished works, the four gospels. We have extensive knowledge of the history at the time the gospel tradition was being formed. It is a mark of the integrity of the gospels that they do not address this painful issue, refraining from placing definitive words in the mouth of Jesus to resolve the debate one way or another.

Conclusion

The percussive impact of Jesus the Teacher, risen from the dead, had historically demonstrable consequences. These include the proclamation of Jesus and the creation of gathered commun-

---

[63] See 1 Cor. 15:3–5, 11.   [64] Gal. 2:5.   [65] Gal. 2:11–14.

[66] For a defence of this understanding as opposed to other opinions of this phrase, see F. F. Bruce, *Commentary on Galatians* (Exeter: Paternoster, 1982), pp. 129–130.

ities of believers, both Jewish and Gentile. This occurred first in Jerusalem and its more immediate surroundings. In time, proclamation was formalized in several apostolates, based on a number of great leaders. Significant strains and controversies arising from the mission work of Paul among the Gentiles, in particular, may be detected.

Less evident but equally real were the gathering, treasuring, forming and finalizing of the gospel traditions. This hidden process occurred throughout a period of great turmoil in Judea, which in turn fuelled the flames of controversy between Paul and his opponents over the inclusion of the Gentiles in the people of God. Yet these events, both in Judea and within the wider community of believers, do not appear to have left any great imprint on the sources of the gospels or the finished gospels. As I will argue, this is due to the commitment of the gospel writers to present Jesus as he was 'back then' and 'back there', that is, within the political and geographical world in which he lived, died and was raised from the dead. The history following Jesus, which he impacted, has not coloured the preservation of the history to which he belonged.

Excursus
The resurrection of Jesus from the dead

The fundamental importance of the resurrection of Jesus from the dead is evident from Paul's words: 'so we [apostles] preach and so you [Corinthians] believed'.[67] The apostles' proclamation of the resurrected one was echoed in the faith of the church.[68]

What is the evidence that Jesus was so raised? On the one hand there is circumstantial evidence, based on probability, and on the other, there is a lack of a plausible alternative.[69]

It can be shown from the letters that, in the immediate aftermath of Jesus' lifespan, there were 'churches' of Jews[70] in Judea who worshipped him in Aramaic as *Mara*, 'Lord',[71] formulated a creed asserting that he 'was raised on the third

---

[67] 1 Cor. 15:11.   [68] *Cf.* 1 Thes. 4:14.
[69] For discussion, with literature, see G. R. Osborne in *DJG*, pp. 673–688, and L. J. Kreitzer in *DPL*, pp. 805–812.
[70] Gal. 1:13, 22; 1 Thes. 2:14.   [71] 1 Cor. 16:22.

day',[72] and were glad that the converted Paul was now 'preaching the faith he once tried to destroy'.[73] According to C. F. D. Moule, 'the coming into existence of the Nazarenes' is a 'phenomenon undeniably attested by the New Testament'.[74] This must have required what Moule calls 'a tremendous confirmatory event'.[75] Jesus was not venerated by them as a martyred teacher, but worshipped and preached as a risen Lord. Remarkable, doubtless, as Jesus was, these communities of 'faith' would not have been formed had he not been raised from the dead.

The members of this community did not discontinue their adherence to Judaism. The set hours for prayer continued to be observed.[76] Eating with Gentiles was not permitted; it required a vision to free Peter to do this.[77] But the zeal for Yahweh of these Jews was now a secondary zeal, qualified by the fact of Jesus' resurrection. Their primary zeal was for the risen Jesus. Even under threat of punishment they would not be silenced.[78] Jesus' resurrection remains the most plausible explanation for the undeniable phenomenon of these Jewish churches and the public witness of their leaders to that resurrection immediately after Jesus' death. According to their opponents, they 'filled the city' with that teaching.[79]

The earliest letters by Paul, written in the early 50s, assume without discussion that both the writer and the readers believed that Jesus had been raised from the dead.[80] Indeed, Paul simply appeals to their certainty about Jesus' historical resurrection as something to clinch his argument about their coming future resurrection, which some of them were doubting.[81] It was because Christ had been raised that they would certainly be raised.[82] Here Paul appeals to the pre-formed tradition which was the instrument of their creation as a church, a tradition which he himself had received from the witnesses of the resurrection.[83]

Critical to the pre-formed tradition of the Jerusalem church

---

[72] 1 Cor. 15:4.   [73] Gal. 1:22.
[74] *The Phenomenon of the New Testament* (London: SCM, 1967), p. 3.
[75] *Ibid.*, p. 17.   [76] Acts 3:1; 10:9.   [77] Acts 10:9–16.
[78] Acts 4:20; 5:29–32.   [79] Acts 5:28.   [80] See *e.g.* 1 Thes. 1:10; 4:14.
[81] 1 Cor. 15:12.   [82] 1 Cor. 15:23.
[83] 1 Cor. 15:1–8; *cf.* Gal. 1:18–19.

cited by Paul is that Christ was entombed.[84] The reality of his death is thereby asserted. But the list of the people to whom Christ ('raised on the third day') 'appeared', when read with his *burial*, implies that the tomb was empty. The one who had died and been entombed was not there.

This is more directly stated in each of the gospels.[85] On the first day of the week, when the women came to attend further to the body, they found the tomb to be empty. This 'first day' tradition must be regarded as secure since it is found in the texts of Mark and John, which were written independently of each other. Moreover, the Jews' 'stolen body' explanation presumes the tomb's emptiness.[86] Both the convinced and the hostile held the tomb to be empty; empty it must have been.

Thus the 'first day' empty-tomb traditions of the women intersect with the 'third day' appearances tradition of the Jerusalem church repeated by Paul to the Corinthians.[87] Jesus had died and been entombed. But the tomb was empty; Jesus appeared alive from the dead on many occasions, to some hundreds of people.

Various explanations have been attempted. For example, it has been maintained that the disciples stole the body, that the women went to the wrong tomb, that another person was crucified by mistake, that Jesus revived in the tomb, or that the disciples had merely a vision or visions of a resurrected Lord. But there is no historical consensus as to the most likely explanation.

The view held by many contemporary scholars, that the disciples were subject to some kind of visionary experiences, is hard to accept. Two people sharing one bed seldom have the same dream. The proposal that between five and six hundred people on twelve or so separate occasions over forty days had the same visionary experience is extremely unlikely.[88]

In any case 'resurrection from the dead', a Jewish concept, literally means, 'standing up in the midst of corpses' (*anastasis nekrōn*). A resurrection which was not bodily is self-contradictory

---

[84] *Etaphē*, 1 Cor. 15:4.

[85] Mt. 28:1–6; Mk. 16:1–6; Lk. 24:1–3; Jn. 20:1–3.   [86] Mt. 28:11–15.

[87] *Cf.* Acts 10:40 where the phrase 'raised on the third day' is spoken by Peter.

[88] See further P. W. Barnett, *The Truth about Jesus* (Sydney: Aquila, 1994), pp. 142–144.

and has been likened to a circle which is square. The various subjective or visionary theories of resurrection are culturally contradictory.

There is only one serious alternative explanation. It is that the disciples stole the body and proclaimed Jesus to have been raised from the dead. In other words, it was a deception, a hoax. A number of objections may be raised against this hypothesis. Apart from the unlikelihood that the perpetrators would call a gospel based on deceit the 'word of truth' and repeatedly call for truthful behaviour among believers, such a theory is difficult to reconcile with subsequent apostolic history. Through the pages of the New Testament we are able to trace the ministries of Peter, James and Paul, the leaders of various mission groups, from the time of the resurrection to their martyr-deaths. This is a period of about three decades. It is implausible that all three would have maintained the deception throughout those years and then gone to their deaths without exposing a hoax. Moreover, there was more than a little friction between these men. Had the resurrection not been true, it is likely that one or other of these strong personalities would have broken ranks to expose the others.

Chapter Seven

From Jesus to gospel text

The ministry span of Jesus ended in AD 33. Some decades later the gospels were published. But by what means or process did the gospels come to be written during this 'in between' period? Moreover, is it true, as is often claimed, that the gospels are quite remote in time and human contact from Jesus, written by people who knew nothing of him?

Apostolic history

As we have seen, without recourse to the Acts of the Apostles, it is possible to catch a glimpse of the apostolates which were the means by which the gospel was spread. Galatians is valuable in this regard. Through the window provided by Galatians 2:7–9 we are able to see what happened in the fifteen years between Jesus and the meeting in Jerusalem in about AD 47:

> When they saw that I had been entrusted with the gospel to the uncircumcised, just as Peter had been entrusted with the gospel to the circumcised (for he who worked through Peter for the mission[1] to the circumcised worked through me also for the Gentiles), and when they perceived the grace given to me, James, Peter and John, who were reputed to be pillars, gave to me and Barnabas the right hand of fellowship, that we should go to the Gentiles and they to the circumcised . . .

This passage is highly informative. First, we learn that the 'pillars' of the Jerusalem church are now James, Peter and John, James being the senior 'pillar' (his name appears first in

---

[1] Literally, 'apostolate', *apostolē*.

Galatians 2:9, pointing to priority of honour). Secondly, almost from the beginning (that is, from *c.* AD 34) there had been two apostolates, one recognized, led by Peter, to the Jews; the other, unrecognized until *c.* AD 47, led by Paul, to the uncircumcised.[2] Thirdly, at the meeting in Jerusalem, agreement was made that Paul should go to the Gentiles. Fourthly, it was then agreed that the three Jerusalem 'pillars' should go to the circumcised. Although this could be interpreted as a corporate 'going', equally it could refer to James, Peter and John each going individually. Although there is no evidence that James travelled beyond Palestine (including Galilee), 'brothers of the Lord' did visit Corinth.[3] Peter certainly, and John probably, travelled far afield in their ministries. In time the two apostolates, of the era *c.* AD 33–47, became four.[4] In my view, almost all the literature of the New Testament, its letters and gospels, issued from these four apostolates.

What were the methods, the missionary practices, of these apostolates?

Mission colleagues and mission letters

From Paul's letters and from Acts we learn that Paul's practice was that after a congregation had been established, he soon moved on to ministry elsewhere. Where difficulties arose, he dispatched a letter carried by an envoy, who probably had a special role in explaining the letter and dealing with problems. For example, Titus had a particular ministry with the Corinthians, and Timothy with the Ephesians. Indeed, Paul surrounded himself with colleagues, whether amanuenses, co-senders of letters, envoys, proxy evangelists (like Epaphras in the Lycus region)[5] or workers sent on ahead (like Timothy and Erastus to Macedonia).[6]

James, Peter and John also had colleagues. James does not

---

[2] Based on Gal. 2:1, 7–9, where the missionary agreement was made fourteen years after Paul's Damascus road experience, which took place about a year after the first Easter.

[3] 1 Cor. 9:5.

[4] This is not to imply that there were no other missions or mission groups associated with the apostles and other Christian leaders. The literature of the NT, however, does seem to be particularly connected with the four missions.

[5] Col. 1:7.   [6] Acts 19:22.

name any in his letter, though he is associated in Jerusalem with his 'brothers' in the 40s[7] and surrounded by the 'elders' (of the church?) in the 50s.[8] Peter had an amanuensis, Silvanus, and a surrogate son, Mark.[9] John's gospel has a postscript from a group who affirm that '*we* know that his testimony is true'. Demetrius was some kind of envoy between John and his churches.[10] The seven churches addressed in the book of Revelation each have an 'angel', who may be a human messenger (Greek *angelos*, 'messenger') summoned by John on Patmos to take the book to the churches.[11]

The evidence of the New Testament points to a number of apostolates or mission teams, led by a recognized figure, which engaged in evangelism and church establishment. The literature of the New Testament, both letters and gospels, was written by members of those apostolates for the benefit of the constituent churches.

Paul's letters are both personal in character and occasional in intent. Nevertheless, their carefully crafted structures and argument suggest that the apostle foresaw an ongoing use and, indeed, dissemination among other churches. Letters, too, were utilized for ministry *in absentia* by James, Peter and John. It should be noted that even Revelation is formally introduced as a letter. Significantly, the letters of James, 1 Peter (and perhaps also John), with Revelation, are each written for a network of churches.[12]

The letters of the New Testament have in common the fact that they are dealing with perceived problems in the churches addressed. Thus letters enjoyed a key role in the care of the churches of the apostolic era. Twenty-two of the twenty-seven documents of the New Testament are letters, which, apart from

[7] Acts 12:17. 'Brothers of the Lord' are mentioned by Paul (1 Cor. 9:5); Jude was a brother of James (Jude 1).

[8] Acts 21:18; *cf.* Acts 15:6.

[9] 1 Pet. 5:12–13.   [10] 3 Jn. 12.   [11] Rev. 2:1, 8, 12, 18; 3:1, 7, 14; *cf.* 1:16.

[12] The letters reveal a changing ministry orientation for Peter and John. Paul and James retained the ministry direction set out at the Jerusalem meeting in *c.* AD 47, Paul to the Gentiles and James to the circumcised. Paul's letters are addressed in the main to Gentiles. The letter of James is written to Jews of the dispersion. 1 Peter, however, suggests that Peter may have shifted his ministry to Gentiles (*cf.* 1:18; 4:3). There is nothing in 1 John to suggest a Jewish readership; his closing words, 'keep yourselves from idols', may have a literal meaning, suggesting Gentile readers.

Hebrews and Jude, seem to be associated with the mission teams led by James, Peter, John and Paul. But this raises a question. If the mission letters were written for the needs of the churches, why were gospels also needed?

Why were gospels needed?

Several of the gospel-writers hint at their reasons for writing. Mark's opening words, 'The beginning of the gospel', tell us that what will follow is the 'gospel' or proclamation *about* (as well as issuing from) 'Jesus Christ, the Son of God'. In the Graeco-Roman world of the time, a gospel (*euangelion*) was an imperial proclamation, usually involving grand and good news.[13] Mark's silence, however, leaves us to infer what his precise reasons for writing were.

Matthew gives no explicit hint at his reason for writing. The readers are left to draw their own conclusions from the contents. The great blocks of Jesus' instruction located within the narrative, together with the final words of Jesus to the disciples, 'Make disciples . . . *teaching* them to observe all that I have commanded you', suggest that Matthew's book is a manual of instruction for believers, based on the teaching of Jesus.

Luke felt impelled to write a consolidated sequential narrative for the benefit of readers symbolized by his addressee, Theophilus.[14] Various shorter and unconnected narratives about Jesus had been 'handed over' to Luke by the original 'ministers and eye-witnesses', but someone must now bring them together for the sake of assured truth about Jesus.

According to John, Jesus performed 'other signs' apart from what he has recorded. Many books could be written about him. It has been necessary to select just some of the 'signs' and write a book about them.[15] In this he has been guided by the purpose, 'that you may believe that Jesus is the Christ, the Son of God, and that believing you may have life in his name'. John's motive in writing is plainly Christological. Although textual uncertainty leaves open the question whether his precise intention is evangelistic ('come to believe') or doctrinal ('believe correctly'),[16] the

---

[13] G. Strecker in *EDNT* 2, p. 69.   [14] Lk. 1:1–4.   [15] Jn. 20:30–31; 21:24.
[16] The text could be either *pisteusēte* (aorist, 'come to believe') or *pisteuēte* (present, 'go on believing').

nature of the discourses and disputes in the gospel makes it almost certain that John's ultimate motive was doctrinal.[17]

Apart from such hints, explicit and implicit, as we find within these texts, there does appear to be an overriding factor in the felt need to write the gospels. Stated briefly, it is that the contemporaries and eye-witnesses of Jesus were beginning to die. The decade of the 60s was critical in this regard. In AD 62, James the brother of the Lord was martyred in Jerusalem. It was probably during AD 65–68 that Peter and Paul were killed in Rome in the pogrom following the great fire in AD 64. The umbilical cord between Jesus and the churches was beginning to be cut. There was the need for records about Jesus written during the lifetimes of those who had been present with the Lord. These would serve to authenticate the Lord in the coming generation, and the next and the next until he returned.

Something like this appears to have been in the minds of Matthew, Luke and John, in particular, though perhaps not Mark. Only Mark describes his work as a gospel (*euangelion*). Briefer, sharper and more provocative than the others, it appears to have been written earlier, with a more strongly evangelistic intent.

Be that as it may, a major reason for the writing of the gospels relates to a sense of growing distance from the Teacher, intensified by the deaths of those who had been with him and who had been eye-witnesses. As I will argue later, the gospels are identifiably biographical. But how had the biographical information about Jesus – his works and words – been retained during these decades of apostolic activity? The answer is to be sought in the religious and educational culture of the Jews of that time, a culture in which Jesus and his followers had been nurtured and which continued with the apostles during the decades between Jesus and the publication of the gospels. This 'rabbinic' religious and educational culture provides the most satisfying model to help understand the means by which, historically, we move from the person of Jesus to the written texts about him.

---

[17] See D. A. Carson, 'The Purpose of the Fourth Gospel: John 20:31 Reconsidered', *JBL* 108 (1987), pp. 639–651, for the argument that this gospel also has an evangelistic intent.

The rabbinic ethos of first-century Judaism[18]

The religious culture to which Jesus and his disciples belonged was 'rabbinic'. By this I mean that rabbis carefully handed over teachings about Judaism to disciples who, in turn, as teachers, delivered the traditions to their disciples, generation by generation.

It was held that the great teachers of the day belonged to a succession that went back, generation by generation, to Moses. Josephus comments that 'the Pharisees have delivered to the people a great many observances by succession from their fathers, which are not written in the law of Moses'.[19] According to the Talmud, 'Moses received Torah from Sinai and delivered it to Joshua, and Joshua to the elders, and the elders to the prophets, and the prophets delivered it to the men of the great synagogue. These said three things: be deliberate in judging, and raise up many disciples, and make a hedge for the Torah.'[20]

Great care was to be taken to 'deliver' the traditions one had received. Rabbi Eliezer ben Hyrcanus declared, 'I have never said in my life a thing that I did not hear from my teachers.'[21] Moreover, the exact recollection of the oral tradition was fundamental. It was said that 'whoever forgets a word of his mishnah, scripture accounts it as if he had lost his soul'.[22]

New Testament writers give evidence of the same tradition-transmission pattern of education and learning. Mark's comment that the people observed the 'tradition of the elders' suggests that this rabbinic culture was current in Jesus' day.[23] The place of the 'traditions' is to be inferred in the accusation against Stephen, that he said Jesus of Nazareth would 'change the customs which Moses delivered to us'.[24] Revealing, too, is Paul's recollection that he had advanced in Judaism beyond

[18] See P. S. Alexander, 'Orality in Pharisaic-Rabbinic Judaism at the Turn of the Eras', in *Jesus and the Oral Gospel Tradition*, ed. H. Wansbrough (Sheffield: JSOT, 1991), pp. 159–184, and R. Riesner, 'Jesus as Preacher and Teacher', in *ibid.*, pp. 185–210.

[19] *Antiquities* xiii.10.6.   [20] *Pirqe 'Aboth* 1.1.

[21] *b. Suk.* 28a, quoted in Alexander, 'Orality in Pharisaic-Rabbinic Judaism', p. 181.

[22] *Pirqe 'Aboth* 3.9.   [23] Mk. 7:3.

[24] Acts 6:14, *allaxei ta ethē ha paredōken hēmin Mōusēs. Cf.* Acts 15:1; 21:21; 22:3; 26:3; 28:17.

many of his own age, so zealous was he 'for the traditions of [his] fathers'.[25]

In the guild of the Pharisees a disciple would learn from a rabbi, as Paul did 'at the feet of Gamaliel'.[26] But the Pharisees also handed over the traditions to the people at large, in particular in the ministry of the synagogue. R. Riesner observes that 'one cannot overstress the importance of the synagogal teaching system as background for the formation and transmission of the gospel tradition. The synagogues provided even in small Galilean villages such as Nazareth a kind of popular education system. Many men could read and write and were used to memorizing and expounding the scriptures.'[27] Jesus and his disciples were born into and nurtured by the powerful religious culture of first-century Judaism.

Rabbi Jesus

As I noted earlier,[28] Jesus was the rabbi or teacher, and the twelve were his disciples. The gospels describe their discipleship in technical rabbinic terminology. They had 'come' to him, 'followed after' him, 'learned from' him and 'taken [his] yoke upon' them.[29] Even a woman was found 'sitting at his feet' like the pupil of a rabbi.[30]

During their time with him the disciples 'received' the 'traditions' which he had 'handed over' to them. That teaching was couched in memorable forms, making use in particular of the parallelism of Hebrew poetry, which, according to Riesner, represents 80% of Jesus' teaching.[31] To parallelism, argues Riesner, must be added other poetical techniques such as alliterations, assonance, rhythm and rhyme, which made Jesus' words 'memorizable', enabling them to be preserved intact.[32]

---

[25] Gal. 1:14.　　[26] Acts 22:3.

[27] Riesner, 'Jesus as Preacher and Teacher', p. 191.

[28] See above, pp. 108–109.　　[29] Mt. 11:28–30; Mk. 1:16–20.

[30] Lk. 10:39.　　[31] Riesner, 'Jesus as Preacher and Teacher', p. 202.

[32] Riesner, *ibid.*, pp. 206–207, rejects the view of W. Kelber, *The Oral and Written Gospel: The Hermeneutics of Speaking and Writing in the Synoptic Tradition, Mark, Paul and Q* (Philadelphia: Fortress, 1983), p. 27, that oral transmission means 'the inevitability of change, flexibility and degrees of improvisation'. Riesner may be correct. His thesis, however, is built on the assumption of the continuity of a rabbinic ethos within early Christianity. In view of the diminishing Jewish and the growing Gentile character of Christianity, the

B. Gerhardsson suggests that Jesus made particular use of aphorisms, which were pre-formulated, to condense his theological teaching into an easily remembered form.[33]

Were Jesus' teachings remembered orally only? There is no reason in principle why one of Jesus' disciples might not have written down his teachings. Matthew, for example, a customs official, was probably sufficiently literate to have been able to make written records of the words of the Teacher. Such a collection of sayings may have been disseminated in the early churches and then included in a gospel in its final form.[34]

This is not to suggest that Jesus fitted the Jewish and rabbinic culture exactly. Unlike rabbis, Jesus took the initiative in disciple-making; *he* called them. Moreover, the rabbi typically would have one pupil; Jesus called twelve. Even more fundamentally, Jesus spoke on his own authority, using 'I say to you' statements, prefixing them with the solemn 'Amen'. He spoke with authority, not like the scribes. J. Neusner, the eminent Jewish scholar of rabbinic traditions, comments, 'No rabbi was so important to rabbinic Judaism as Jesus was to Christianity. None prophesied as an independent authority. None left a category of I-sayings, for none had the prestige to do so.'[35] Going beyond that, Riesner argues that Jesus' Amen-sayings marked his speech out as divinely inspired and revealed him as having messianic authority.[36]

Jesus called his twelve disciples with a view to training them to call Israel to repentance. But they were to go in his name with his message, not their own. The pre-Easter mission to Israel was the prelude to the post-Easter mission to the Gentiles.[37] In the post-Easter situation, where congregations were formed to invoke Jesus as *Mara* ('Lord'), these former pupils became the

---

rabbinic character must have diminished in time.

[33] B. Gerhardsson, 'The Narrative Meshalim in the Synoptic Gospels', *NTS* 34 (1988), pp. 339–363.

[34] *Cf.* Papias as quoted in Eusebius, *Historia Ecclesiastica* III.39.16: 'So then, Matthew compiled the oracles in the Hebrew language but everyone interpreted them as he was able.'

[35] Quoted in Riesner, 'Jesus as Preacher and Teacher', p. 208.

[36] *Ibid.*, p. 209.

[37] M. Hengel, *The 'Hellenization' of Judaea in the First Century after Christ* (London: SCM, 1989), pp. 7–18, suggests that Jesus may have had contacts before Easter with the Jewish Hellenists, for example, Barnabas.

transmitters of the traditions they had received from the Teacher. The converts on the day of Pentecost devoted themselves to the apostles' teaching, which they must have heard first from the Teacher in the recent past.[38] In the first few years, a decade or more before Paul's first missionary journey in about AD 47, churches began to proliferate – Aramaic-speaking churches in Jerusalem, throughout Judea and Galilee; Greek-speaking churches in Caesarea, Ptolemais, Tyre, Sidon and Antioch. There were probably churches, too, in Samaria.[39] The words of the Teacher were taught and held in the memories of the people.

The apostles also formulated various summaries of Jesus' life and death as part of their proclamation of the gospel. We have already noted allusions in the letters to aspects of Jesus' life, both general and specific.[40] Jesus' betrayal, his Last Meal, his death, burial, resurrection and subsequent appearances are set out in two pre-formed traditions (quoted in 1 Corinthians) which Paul had earlier 'received'.[41] Examples of public proclamation exist in summary form in the speeches of Peter recorded in the first ten chapters of Acts.[42]

But it is likely that various narratives and teachings were also soon committed to writing. There is reason to believe that the account of Jesus' arrest, trials and crucifixion, as recorded in Mark, was quickly committed to writing, perhaps lest the details be forgotten.[43] The words spoken on the Mount of Olives may have reached their present written form (or perhaps an earlier draft) at about the time Caligula was threatening to desecrate the temple in AD 40. Whatever the precise details, it is clear that various parts of the 'story' about Jesus came into written existence early. In the prologue of his two-volume work Luke says that '*many* have undertaken to compile a narrative . . .' The

---

[38] Acts 2:42.   [39] Acts 9:31.   [40] See above, pp. 39–57.

[41] 1 Cor. 11:23–26; 15:1–7.

[42] Acts 2:22–36; 3:11–26; 4:8–12; 5:29–32; 10:36–43. See G. N. Stanton, *Jesus of Nazareth in New Testament Preaching* (Cambridge: Cambridge University Press, 1974).

[43] There is no mention in Mark of the name of the high priest before whom Jesus appeared. This would make sense if the writer of the account Mark used wished to avoid antagonizing Caiaphas, the high priest in question. Caiaphas died in AD 37, suggesting that the passion narrative used by Mark appeared before that time. Caiaphas's name is found, however, in Matthew, Luke and Acts and John.

words and works of the teacher were thus current orally, in memorized form, but also in short written accounts.

Rabbinic vocabulary in early Christianity

This vocabulary of Jewish rabbinic culture, now used in a Christian context, occurs at many places in the New Testament. In Matthew's 'Great Commission', Jesus instructs the disciples to 'make disciples' of people from among the nations, or Gentiles. That is, the disciples were to 'teach' these new disciples to 'keep' all that he, the Teacher, had commanded the original disciples.[44] The tradition Jesus had handed over to them they were to hand over to others, who were to receive and keep what they had been taught. This tradition flowed from the Teacher, Jesus of Nazareth, who was now the risen Lord, worshipped by his disciples.

Paul commends the Corinthians because 'you hold to the traditions (*paradoseis*) even as I handed them over to you'[45] – for example, the 'traditions' of the Lord's Supper and the narrative of the death, burial and resurrection of Christ.[46] The second letter to the Corinthians is of particular importance in regard to the biographical information about Jesus which Paul had evidently passed on to the church and to which he appeals without explanatory comment.[47]

Although Paul was not one of the original disciples, he was no less a transmitter of the traditions of the Lord than they.[48] By the Lord's intervention Paul was called an 'apostle', as set out in his careful argument in Galatians 1:3 – 2:10.[49] The authority of the original apostles derived from Christ, but so, too, did Paul's.[50] Nevertheless, Paul does not exercise this authority independently of the 'tradition' he received from those who were apostles before him, or in denial of their apostolicity.

Paul describes evangelism in 'rabbinic' terms. Believers are those who have 'learned Christ', that is, who have 'heard' and 'been taught' and who are now 'walking' according to Christ.[51] This is a new *halakhah*, 'received' from Christ, 'handed over' by Paul and 'received' by believers.

---

[44] Mt. 28:19–20.   [45] 1 Cor. 11:2, my translation.
[46] 1 Cor. 11:23; 15:1–3.   [47] See above, pp. 47–50.   [48] 2 Thes. 2:15.
[49] Gal. 1:11–12, 15–17, 18–19, 21–23; 2:5, 6, 7, 9.   [50] 2 Cor. 10:8; 13:10.
[51] Eph. 4:20–21; *cf.* 1:13. See also 1 Thes. 4:1.

Paul provided for the tradition to be extended by others within his own apostolate. Epaphras, a native of the Lycus region, is described as Paul's proxy minister.[52] Paul had not personally visited that region. The Colossians had 'learned' and been 'taught' the 'gospel' by Epaphras. In the face of false teaching, 'a tradition from men which is not according to Christ', Paul urges them that, as they 'have received Christ Jesus the Lord', so they should continue to 'live in him, rooted and built up in him and established in *the* faith'.[53] Here is 'the tradition', 'the faith', that emanates from Christ, which they have 'learned' and been 'taught', not by Paul, but by Epaphras, a 'faithful minister of Christ'. Those who have received the tradition have 'received Christ Jesus the Lord'. It is no dead tradition, however, but a living one. The gospel, 'the word of Christ, lives among them in their worship as they 'teach . . . one another' in 'psalms and hymns and spiritual songs'.[54] The received tradition, 'the word of Christ', controlled what they sang to each other.

Foreseeing the end of his own life, Paul arranged for the tradition to be passed on into the future. He instructed Timothy, 'What you have heard from me . . . entrust to faithful men who will be able to teach others also.'[55] Timothy had been 'taught' and had 'heard' the body of teaching (the 'what') from Paul, as a pupil from a rabbi. Timothy is now to assume the rabbi's role, in teaching others, to provide for the next generation. The Rule of Faith, its child the Roman Creed, and the Apostles' Creed, in time came to function in the same way.

Paul uses this vocabulary for believers who are the fruits of the ministry of others outside his apostolate, for example the Christians in Rome. He is thankful that they have become obedient from the heart to 'the pattern (*typos*) of teaching' to which they had been 'handed over'.[56] Whereas the usual reference is to 'handing over' a body of teaching to the people, in this case, interestingly, the *people* are 'handed over' to the body of teaching. Near the end of the letter Paul warns the Romans to take note of those who oppose 'the teaching' which they have 'learned'.[57]

---

[52] Col. 1:7.   [53] Col. 1:7; 2:7.   [54] Col. 3:16.   [55] 2 Tim. 2:2.
[56] Rom. 6:17, my translation.   [57] Rom. 16:17, my translation.

Paul often refers to 'doctrine' (*didaskalia*),[58] the body of teaching associated with the tradition going back to Christ. But there was false teaching, doctrine which Paul calls gangrenous, as opposed to 'sound' ('hygienic').[59] Timothy is to be 'a good minister of Christ Jesus, nourished on the words of the faith and of the good [sound] doctrine' which he had 'followed' after.[60]

Although Paul is the chief user of this technical 'rabbinic' vocabulary, it is found across the New Testament. Acts refers to the 'apostles' teaching' (*didachē*).[61] The readers of the letter to the Hebrews, having 'heard' the living word of God, the gospel, ought by now to be teachers of others.[62] Prominent also in Hebrews is the notion of a 'confession', a body of teaching (*homologia*) which the readers were to 'consider' and 'hold fast to'.[63] It is possible that a 'confession', and its antonym 'denial', had roots in the rabbinic language of synagogue culture.[64] 2 John speaks of 'the doctrine (*didachē*) of Christ'. A person who comes from outside is not to be received unless he brings that 'doctrine'.[65] Jude exhorts his readers to struggle for 'the faith' which was once 'handed over' to the saints.[66] Notice that it is *the* faith, once handed over, rabbi-like, by the Lord Jesus to his original followers for which Jude's readers were to contend.[67]

The apostolates and the traditions of Jesus

Broadly speaking, then, early Christianity was spread by a series of interlocking apostolates, those of James, Peter, John and Paul. It appears that the tradition-transmission culture of Judaism, to

---

[58] Rom. 12:7; 15:4.   [59] 1 Tim. 1:10.   [60] 1 Tim. 4:6.   [61] Acts 2:42; 5:38.
[62] Heb. 4:2, 12–13; 5:11–12; 6:1.   [63] Heb. 3:1; 10:23.
[64] O. Hofius in *EDNT* 2, p. 514.   [65] 2 Jn. 9–10.
[66] Jude 3, my translation.
[67] Attention is drawn to a pseudonymous letter of 'Peter' to James in the (second-century?) *Pseudo-Clementine Homilies*, to be found in *New Testament Apocrypha*, ed. E. Hennecke and W. Schneemelcher, quoted in A. I. Baumgarten, 'Literary Evidence for Jewish Christianity', in *The Galilee of Late Antiquity*, ed. L. I. Levine (Cambridge, MA: Harvard University Press, 1992), p. 43, n. 25. Addressed as this work is to James the bishop of the church, 'Peter' urges that the Gentiles should not 'receive' the books of Peter's preachings; only to fellow Jews who have been found worthy may these books be 'handed over'. The provenance, which is clearly Jewish-Christian, is most probably Galilee (so Baumgarten, p. 50). The culture is that of tradition and transmission, evocative of the vocabulary of the apostle Paul.

which Jesus belonged, carried on for a period into these apostolates. The apostolic leaders became the focal points for the holding and transmission of the teaching and the deeds of Jesus, their teacher and Messiah. Thus the tradition-transmission culture of Judaism to which Jesus belonged and which carried over into early Christianity was a culture conducive to treasuring various accounts, oral and written, of the Teacher. The eventual writing of the gospels represents the end point of a process begun by Jesus' own ministry.

Qualifications of the tradition-transmission model

Neat though this explanatory model is, there are a number of qualifications.[68] It may be noticed, first, that Paul does not confine tradition to the oral. 'So then, brothers,' he tells the Thessalonians, 'stand firm and hold to the traditions which you were taught by us, either by word of mouth or *by letter.*'[69] The authority which the Lord gave Paul to build up the churches was exercised by letter as well as in person,[70] something to which the Corinthians took exception.[71] 'Eye-witnesses and ministers of the word' handed over to Luke their written narratives, out of which Luke created his own consolidated, sequential account.[72] Clearly the rabbinic culture of early Christianity accepted written traditions as well as oral.[73] In any case, the variations between the four gospels suggest that the rote memorizing of some rabbinic circles was not practised by the disciples of Jesus. Perhaps this was because, on the one hand, they were less literate than the disciples of the rabbinic

---

[68] See B. Witherington, *The Christology of Jesus* (Minneapolis: Fortress, 1990), pp. 16–22, for a critique of Kelber's preference for orality over written texts. It is noted that the Qumran community received both oral and written words as authoritative and may reasonably (against Kelber) serve as a parallel to early Christianity. Moreover, that Christians were 'a people of the book' is amply illustrated by the place given to the OT.

[69] 2 Thes. 2:15.   [70] 2 Cor. 13:10; 12:19; *cf.* 1 Cor. 14:37.

[71] 2 Cor. 10:8–11.   [72] Lk. 1:1–4.

[73] There is no reason to believe that the Jewish tradition was confined to the oral. At some point the teachings of the rabbis must have been committed to writing for their collation and inclusion in the Mishnah.

academies in Jerusalem, and, on the other, Jesus did not stand in a learned rabbinic succession.[74]

Again, there was a certain fluidity between the apostolates. Both Silvanus/Silas and John Mark worked with different leaders. Each began as a member of the Jerusalem church, under the headship of James. Each worked at different times with Paul. Both men worked within Peter's fellowship. These 'crossovers' inevitably diminished the tight continuities there may otherwise have been.

Somewhat connected with the interchange of co-workers was the sharing of a number of traditions and teachings. For instance, Paul and Peter share the use of the introductory benediction.[75] Likewise, the theme of a wife's submission to her husband is common to the letters of Peter and Paul.[76] Moreover, there are points of paraenetic contact evident between 1 Peter and James.[77] 1 Peter also has material found in the letters to the Romans, Ephesians and Hebrews.[78] The strands of tradition and paraenesis are not hermetically sealed within the apostolates.

Perhaps of greater importance was the increasing resistance of Jewish audiences to the gospel of Christ. The writing of Acts cannot have been very distant in time from its closing scene in Rome. In words of pathos the author makes it clear that the future of the gospel lies with the Gentiles; the Jews will not listen. As the Jews decrease, so the Gentiles will increase. Inevitably the rabbinic-Jewish culture of tradition transmission must have been weakened, the more so as relationships between Jews and Christians deteriorated in the decades following.[79] Likewise, the apostolates of Peter and John, located as they were among Gentiles, probably became more directed towards Gentiles. 1 Peter and the gospel of John are saturated with Jewish imagery, but in their received form they are written with Gentiles in mind. For example, Peter writes to readers as 'exiles

---

[74] Acts 4:13; cf. Jn. 7:15.   [75] 2 Cor. 1:3–7; Eph. 1:3–10; 1 Pet. 1:3.

[76] See e.g. 1 Cor. 14:33–34; 1 Pet. 3:1.

[77] Jas. 1:2/1 Pet. 1:6; Jas. 4:7/1 Pet. 5:6–9; Jas. 4:10/1 Pet. 5:6.

[78] See J. N. D. Kelly, The Epistles of Peter and Jude (London: A. and C. Black, 1969), pp. 11–12.

[79] This does not appear to have been adequately accounted for in B. Chilton, Profiles of a Rabbi (Atlanta: Scholars, 1989), in his attack on source and redaction criticism, in favour of a rabbinic milieu as an exclusive explanation for the creation of the synoptic gospels.

of the Dispersion', as if they are Jews, but it is clear that he is thinking of them as 'Jews' in a merely symbolic sense; they have been redeemed in a spiritual exodus.[80] John must explain that 'rabbi' means 'teacher', 'Messiah' means 'Christ' and 'Cephas' means 'Peter'.[81] He speaks of Passover and Tabernacles as 'feasts of the Jews',[82] which implies a Gentile readership.

In short, orality came to an end. The letters of the apostles were obviously authoritative in the churches and they were *written*. The diminishing Jewish influence within early Christianity and the 'turning to the Gentiles' must also have contributed to the eventual decline of orality. Not least, the tradition emanated from Jesus; it was his person and his teaching which were unique. He was not one teacher among many; the apostolic leaders were transmitters and interpreters of *his* tradition.[83] In an era when the eye-witnesses, including the apostolic leaders, began to leave the scene, it became critical that the oral and written traditions about Jesus should be established in permanent form, taking their place with the letters and forming a canon of the new covenant to be attached to the literature of the old covenant as its fulfilment. The people of the new Israel were to be, like Israel, a people of the book.

From tradition to gospels

Authorities from the second century establish that four gospels were recognized by the church.[84] The titles attached in our earliest manuscripts, 'According to Matthew', and so on, imply that there was one gospel of the Lord Jesus Christ expressed in four gospels, 'according to' four different writers.

The names of the authors may be significant. Spurious gospels of later centuries were attached to the names of known disciples of the Lord, especially to Peter and Thomas, who are prominent

---

[80] 1 Pet. 1:1. In 1 Pet. 2:12; 4:3 'Gentiles' is used in the light of Christian believers' being the elect people of God (2:9–10). 'Gentiles' is metaphorical for what the readers once were, and what people around them still are, namely, unbelievers. Therefore, it need not imply that the readers are Jews. See 1 Pet. 1:1, 18–21; 2:11–12; *cf.* 4:3–4.

[81] Jn. 1:38, 41, 42.   [82] Jn. 5:1; *cf.* 2:13; 7:2.   [83] *Cf.* Col. 2:8.

[84] See M. Hengel, *Studies in the Gospel of Mark* (London: SCM, 1985), pp. 64–84, for argument in favour of the earliness of the attribution of the titles of the four gospels.

in the canonical gospels by word or action. Only one of the four canonical gospels, however (the fourth), is written by a well-known disciple. The first, 'according to Matthew', is also by one of the twelve, but he is not prominent, being referred to only a few times in the gospels. Mark and Luke were not original disciples, nor were they mission leaders, but mere co-workers. The identities of the gospel authors, apart from John, prove to be rather unexpected, a factor which supports the probability of authenticity.

But when were they written? Apart from the obvious fact that they must have been written after Jesus' death in AD 33 and before AD 100, when they begin to be quoted, there is no consensus among scholars as to date of authorship. It is likely that Matthew and Luke were written after and dependent upon Mark, and that John is independent of the others (whether earlier or later is debated). Various attempts at dating the gospels by external events – the deaths of Peter and Paul under Nero in AD 65–68, the destruction of the temple in AD 70, the curse on the Nazarenes as from the Council of Jamnia in the 80s – while interesting exercises, have proved inconclusive.[85] Some argue that because the gospels and Acts do not mention the death of Peter and Paul or the destruction of the temple, they must have been written before AD 65 or 70. But this is to argue from silence. And the Benediction of the Council of Jamnia does not excommunicate the Nazarenes from the synagogues, but pronounces a curse upon them. So while references to synagogue excommunication in John[86] make good historical sense in the time of Jesus, they are not explained (as some have argued) as a reaction to the Benediction.

By what process were the gospels written? Here we are on rather firmer ground, at least with the two by the non-apostles, Mark and Luke. Papias, a second-century authority, describes how Mark was written; Luke himself tells us the process by which he wrote. Despite differences, Mark and Luke were written in what we might call a Jewish tradition-transmission ethos. According to Papias, Mark, who had not heard the Lord, was Peter's *hermēneutēs*, 'interpreter', writing down in his gospel what he had heard Peter say.[87] Jesus instructed Peter, Mark heard

---

[85] See E. E. Ellis, 'Dating the New Testament', *NTS* 26 (1980), pp. 487–488.
[86] Jn. 9:23; 12:42; 16:2.   [87] Eusebius, *Historia Ecclesiastica* III.39.14.

Peter, and Mark wrote down the tradition of the Lord.

We should note that Papias also refers to the living tradition as continuing beyond the apostolic age. As Bishop of Hierapolis in the province of Asia in the first decades of the second century, Papias had opportunities to meet and enquire of followers of the first disciples, Andrew, Peter, Philip, Thomas, James, John and Matthew. For his part, Papias preferred the 'living voice' of the Lord, which he heard from these men, to what was written in books.[88]

The other non-apostle, Luke, explains that he had been in contact with those who 'from the beginning were eye-witnesses and ministers of the word', that is, original disciples of Jesus.[89] Some of these had written 'narratives' of aspects of Jesus' ministry, which they 'handed over' (a rabbinic term) to Luke. He subsequently consolidated these narratives into one consecutive 'narrative'.

In the cases of Mark and Luke there is the Jewish tradition-transmission ethos, Mark's oral, Luke's written. This appears to be in line with a rabbinic-tradition theory. There are qualifications, however. Mark had also been Paul's assistant, and Luke's written narratives probably were handed over to him by original eye-witnesses, that is, from non-Pauline sources. The model of an isolated and enclosed apostolate as a cipher back to the Teacher is not true to the facts.

According to the gospel of John its author had been witness to the signs, teaching and death of Christ.[90] The text specifically states that the 'disciple whom Jesus loved' was this witness and wrote the gospel.[91] Added to the 'beloved disciple's' own eye-witness claim is the affidavit of the community with him, 'We know that his witness is true.'[92] In this case the 'tradition' from the Teacher was 'received by' John and attested by those who were instructed by John; they knew his witness was true. The gospel 'according to John' is the most detail-specific of the four

---

[88] Quoted in *ibid.*, III.39.4.   [89] Lk. 1:1–4.

[90] Jn. 1:14; 2:11; 19:35; 1 Jn. 1:1–3.

[91] Jn. 21:20, 24. It is clear, by process of elimination, that the beloved disciple must be John Zebedee; see Jn. 21:2; *cf.* 13:23–24. This is the view of Irenaeus and other second-century authorities.

[92] Jn. 21:24.

gospels.[93] Its precision regarding place names and topography of both Galilee and Judea is consistent with its author's having been an eye-witness and companion to Jesus (though many dispute this).[94]

The first gospel was attributed by second-century authorities to Matthew. This Matthew must be the apostle of that name, who appears in the list of the twelve apostles in the gospel of Matthew.[95] Based on references in the gospel of Mark, this Matthew is to be identified as Levi, the tetrarch's customs collector from Capernaum, whom Jesus called to follow him.[96] Possibly his full name was Matthew the Levite, son of Alphaeus.[97]

Judea and Galilee, the world of Matthew's gospel where Jesus comes before us, is an exclusively Jewish world. In this gospel, practices unique to Jews are referred to, but not explained. For the duration of his ministry Jesus and his disciples were to 'go nowhere among the Gentiles' but to confine themselves to the 'lost sheep of the house of Israel'.[98] Only after the resurrection are the apostles to go outside Israel to the Gentiles to make disciples.[99] Culturally speaking, Matthew's is the most Jewish of the four gospels, written, so it appears, for Jewish Christian readers.

[93] See E. F. Meyers and J. F. Strange, *Archaeology, the Rabbis and Early Christianity* (London: SCM, 1981), p. 160.

[94] J. A. T. Robinson, *Redating The New Testament* (London: SCM, 1976), p. 11, came to the view that the author was himself the source of what he wrote. Robinson departed from his earlier agreement with C. H. Dodd, *Historical Tradition in the Fourth Gospel* (Cambridge: Cambridge University Press, 1963), who argued that the underlying sources were primitive to the situation narrated, but from another source. J. D. G. Dunn, 'John and the Oral Tradition', in *Jesus and the Oral Gospel Tradition*, ed. H. Wansbrough (Sheffield: JSOT, 1991), pp. 351–379, endorses and confirms the view of C. H. Dodd. Dunn notes Robinson's view, but does not interact further with him.

[95] Mt. 10:3.   [96] Mt. 9:9; *cf.* Mk. 2:14–17.

[97] Matthew's own role in the writing of the gospel bearing his name is uncertain. Various underlying sources have been identified, including the gospel of Mark, which supplies the basic narrative of events. Inserted into this framework are teachings of Jesus derived from collections now called 'Q' and 'M'. It is possible that Matthew had also been responsible for compiling one or other of these earlier sayings collections. Papias states that Matthew 'compiled the oracles [of the Lord] in the Hebrew language'. The universal tradition of the second century attributing the first gospel to Matthew suggests that Matthew wrote the finished work.

[98] Mt. 10:5–6; but *cf.* 15:21–34.   [99] Mt. 28:19.

The gospel of Matthew appears to place great emphasis on Galilee. This is understandable, since Matthew began to follow Jesus in Capernaum in Galilee. According to Matthew, it was when Jesus began his ministry in Capernaum, in 'Galilee of the Gentiles', that God shone his great light for the sake of the Gentiles who sat in darkness and the shadow of death.[100] It was from Galilee that the apostles were to take the gospel of the risen Christ to the nations (or Gentiles).[101] From Matthew's perspective, Galilee is the centre for the world mission to the nations.[102] In my view, this gospel is written out of and for a Jewish Christian community in Galilee.[103]

Peter, too, enjoys a special place in this gospel,[104] perhaps reflecting the possibility that Galilee was evangelized as part of Peter's apostolate to the circumcised.[105] After his escape from Herod Agrippa in about AD 41, Peter went to 'another place'.[106] Since Peter is back in Jerusalem about AD 47, the most logical location for that 'other place' would have been his native Galilee, close at hand, yet safe.[107]

Was Matthew connected with James's apostolate to Jews? Apart from the letter of James's considerable dependence on Matthew, or an earlier source or version of Matthew,[108] there is no direct evidence connecting Matthew with James. James was clearly the leader of the Jerusalem church, however, and therefore he would have enjoyed a primacy among the Jewish churches of Judea and Galilee. Moreover, James was a Galilean. But above all, he was the brother of the Lord, something that must have added to his standing in the community of faith.

---

[100] Mt. 4:15–17.   [101] Mt. 28:16–20.   [102] Mt. 4:24–25.

[103] So, too, but on other grounds, A. J. Saldarini, 'The Gospel of Matthew and Jewish-Christian Conflict', in *The Galilee of Late Antiquity*, ed. L. I. Levine (Cambridge, MA: Harvard University Press, 1992), pp. 23–38.

[104] Especially Mt. 16:13–20.

[105] Gal. 2:8; *cf.* Acts 9:31–32; 12:17; *cf.* R. Bauckham, *Jude and the Relatives of Jesus in the Early Church* (Edinburgh: T. and T. Clark, 1990), pp. 131–133, for the suggestion that both the relatives of Jesus as well as numbers of the original disciples became prominent in the church of Galilee.

[106] Acts 12:17.

[107] E. E. Ellis, 'The Date and Provenance of Mark's Gospel', in *The Four Gospels 1992*, II, ed. F. Van Segbroeck (Leuven: Leuven University Press, 1992), p. 813, proposes Caesarea as the 'other place'. But Peter would have been less safe in Gentile Caesarea, the domicile of his persecutor, Agrippa.

[108] See above, p. 150.

Matthew's very Jewish gospel, with a special interest in Galilee and Peter, may well locate the author among the churches of Galilee, that is, within the general sphere of James's influence.

From tradition to text via living links

The milieu of early Christianity in which the letters and the gospels were written was 'rabbinic'. Moreover, the movement was concentrated in a number of missionary apostolates, with constituent churches. Certainly there was some 'crossover' of co-workers from one group to another, with accompanying interchange of teaching. The 'tradition' was not only oral; written texts were 'handed over' to Luke. Nevertheless, the literature arose in an ethos of rabbinic tradition, channelled in various apostolates.

The ascription in the second century of the four gospels to Matthew, Mark, Luke and John places each of these writers in living contact with the Teacher. In the case of Matthew and John the contact was direct, with no intermediaries. Mark was at one remove from Jesus, joined to him by Peter. Luke, too, was at one remove from Jesus, linked to him by those eye-witnesses and ministers who 'handed over' their written traditions to him.

The gospels have come to us by a two-stage process comprising *tradition*, the 'handing over' of various 'traditions' about Jesus both oral and written; and *redaction*, the process of committing to writing the finished work. The genre chosen by the writers was the *bios*, the biography; the subject matter was the *person*.[109] The writers were not mere editors, on the one hand, or freely creative authors, on the other.[110] Rather, they were controlled by an interest in biographical history. Moreover, they were not historically distant from Jesus, but were either eye-

[109] So R. A. Burridge, *What are the Gospels?* (Cambridge: Cambridge University Press, 1992), pp. 256–259.

[110] The source critics tended to see the evangelists as 'scissors and paste' editors of the pre-existing sources. While some redaction critics have adopted a conservative approach to the role of the redactors, others have seen them as quite creative in the freedoms taken in manipulating the tradition with which they have worked. For a critique of the unfettered approach in redaction criticism, see D. A. Carson, 'Redaction Criticism', in *Scripture and Truth*, ed. D. A. Carson and J. D. Woodbridge (Grand Rapids: Baker, rev. edn. 1995), pp. 119–142.

witnesses (Matthew and John) or dependent on those who were (Mark and Luke). Both elements, tradition and redaction, are favourable to an authentic final product. The tradition was transmitted in a culture in which there was the accurate 'handing over' of information. The redaction was in a form, the *bios*, which at that time took historical facts seriously. The redactors were connected with the person Jesus about whom they wrote, either immediately and directly, or at only one remove from him. Thus the gospels are not distant, dry texts, severed from the Teacher. Rather, they are living texts, connected to Jesus by those who were with him, and who had served him in the years before the gospels were finally written.

The classification of the gospels as *bioi* does not mean that they lacked underlying assumptions or authorial intent, any more than other *bioi* of those times lacked these things. The various confessions of, for example, the centurion in Mark, Peter in Matthew, Mary in Luke or Thomas in John, appear to seek a similar response from those who heard the gospel read. This does not alter the hypothesis that these documents are by genre *bioi*.

The function of the apostolic letters

We must recognize a difference in function between the letters and the gospels. The letters of the New Testament are pastoral documents written for the ordering and correction of the churches according to the tradition of Jesus. With one or two exceptions they emanate from the various apostolates, those led by James, Peter, John and Paul.

The content of the letters is remarkably varied. Nevertheless, right thinking about Christ is a major theme. This in turn touches on relationships within the churches, between the churches and between the members of the churches and the wider society.[111] The letters mirror the situations the apostles faced in day-to-day ministry. The distant figures of strong-minded but wayward church members, as well as seductive, intruding false teachers, can be discerned, silhouetted, as it were, between the lines. Exterior to the churches, but sharply impinging on them, is a hostile indigenous culture, whether

[111] See above, pp. 134–137.

Jewish or Gentile. In very many cases the letters assume that the churches are under dire threat to their survival.

As a generalization it can be said that the letters are the application of the tradition of Christ by the apostles to the variety and diversity of circumstances which the churches at that time faced. Each letter arises out of and addresses those circumstances. The breadth of application and subject matter is quite complex. But, as we shall see, the gospels are much more focused, concentrating their contents on the words and works of Jesus of Nazareth. This narrow band of interest is in strong contrast with the breadth of concern of the letters.[112]

The gospels reflect an ethos of Jesus 'back there'

Whatever else they are (and the debate about gospel definition continues to rage),[113] the gospels are biographical. Their writers had a more focused goal than the letter-writers. The gospel-writers wrote about Jesus. One has only to compare Luke's gospel with the letters of his colleague Paul, or John's gospel with his own letters, or Mark's gospel with 1 Peter, to see the point.

This holds true even for those parts of the gospels setting out the teaching of Jesus. With few exceptions,[114] the teachings relate to the circumstances of the people of Galilee and Judea in the 30s. They are not concerned with the issues of later decades

---

[112] According to Burridge, *What are the Gospels?*, 'Paul's choice of the genre of the epistle may have been to communicate to a community some distance away, but it is a genre which is amenable for dealing with a specific event, issue or doctrine; *bios* (*i.e.* biography), on the other hand, deals with a specific person' (pp. 256–257).

[113] Burridge, *ibid.*, pp. 191–239, concludes that the gospels, including the fourth gospel, were in their cultural environment recognizably *bioi Iēsou*, biographies of Jesus.

[114] Jesus' teaching about righteousness in regard to the law and the prophets (Mt. 5:17–20) may be an example where a controversy in the early church (reflected in Galatians, Romans and James) is echoed in the words of Jesus. But are Jesus' words anachronistic or (more probably) are they genuinely historical, in their own way helping to precipitate the controversy of the coming years? In favour of their genuineness is the insistence on the preservation in their entirety of the law and the prophets (Mt. 5:18), an insistence which finds no counterpart in Paul's letters.

and other locations which the writers of the letters address. The furious debate over 'the truth of the gospel'[115] (that is, what is to be required of the Gentiles for their inclusion in the people of God) is a good example. This debate dominated the 50s and 60s and involved the great apostolic leaders James, Peter and Paul, yet Luke does not put into Jesus' mouth any teaching that would resolve the matter along the lines of his colleague Paul's views.

The gospel of John betrays knowledge unparalleled in the synoptic gospels of the geography and topography of both Galilee and Judea. Historically, John's account of the interplay between the Roman governor and the chief priests reveals an acute awareness of the political circumstances of Judea during Pontius Pilate's tenure. For whom did John write his *bios* (biography) of Jesus? The numerous explanations of Hebrew terms[116] as well as geographic[117] and religious details[118] suggest that this gospel was not written for the people of Galilee and Judea, or indeed for Jewish readers.[119] John is writing for people outside of the frame of time and space that Jesus originally occupied. His readers were not 'there and then'; they were 'here and now', whenever and wherever that was.[120] But John's *bios* informs them about Jesus and his world of 'there and then', which they did not know.

Christologically, too, John makes this distinction. He distinguishes between his own post-Easter perspectives and the pre-Easter circumstances of Jesus' ministry.[121] To be sure, John establishes his own exalted view of the Word in the prologue, and Jesus' actions and utterances throughout are described in light of that view. Yet Jesus' teaching discourses are chiefly about the Father, and rather obliquely about himself. Even with John's use of the post-Easter term 'Lord', the distinction between 'then' and 'now' is preserved. John describes a few pre-Easter

---

[115] Gal. 2:5, 14; see above pp. 126–127.

[116] 1:38, 41, 42; 19:13, 17; 20:16.   [117] 3:23; 4:4; 6:1; 12:21; 18:13, 28.

[118] 7:37; 10:22; 19:31.   [119] 2:6; 2:13; 5:1; 7:2; 11:55.

[120] See further D. A. Carson, 'Understanding Misunderstandings in the Fourth Gospel', *TB* 33 (1982), pp. 58–89.

[121] See E. E. Lemcio, *The Past of Jesus in the Gospels* (Cambridge: Cambridge University Press, 1991), pp. 91–106; M. M. Thompson, 'The Historical Jesus and the Johannine Jesus', in *Exploring the Gospel of John*, ed. R. A. Culpepper and C. C. Black (Louisville: Westminster John Knox, 1996), pp. 3–17.

actions by the 'Lord' with post-Easter overtones,[122] but more frequently it is a respectful term of address, consistent with the historical situation.[123] Jesus' own words, 'You call me Teacher and Lord; and . . . so I am',[124] are congruent with that disciple-to-teacher reverence. Apart from Thomas's post-Easter confession ('My Lord and my God'), the people who encounter the pre-Easter Jesus, as well as the disciples, struggle to articulate the truth about him which is revealed to the reader in the prologue. Even Peter's confession that Jesus is the 'Holy One of God'[125] says as much about God as it does about Jesus.

In short, notwithstanding his pre-incarnation and post-Easter perspectives on Jesus, John preserves a sense of history. The readers, who have been told who Jesus is, watch through a one-way glass as the people of the day struggle unsuccessfully, or with only partial success, to identify him.

This 'past of Jesus' is even more pronounced in the synoptic gospels. Mark, in particular, portrays Jesus ministering at lakeside Capernaum, living with and being followed by, among others, fishermen from the Lake of Galilee. Another disciple, Levi, was a Capernaum-based customs collector for Herod the tetrarch, whose capital, Tiberias, was just a few miles down the lakeside. Travel across into neighbouring Hellenistic regions was easy at that time, but would not have been so after the 60s, when relationships between Jews and Gentiles deteriorated in that region.[126] In other words, the synoptics, though (in the case of Mark and Luke) probably written outside Palestine, nevertheless present their accounts of Jesus entirely consistently with the geography and politics of Jesus' world in Jesus' times.

The distinction between 'then' and 'now' appears to be important for Mark. For example, his throwaway words, 'Thus he declared all meats clean' and 'Let the reader understand', are deliberate momentary flights from the history of Jesus *then* to the situation of the reader *now*.[127] They serve to strengthen our sense of the author's desire to present a Jesus situated in those times and at that place.

[122] 4:3; 6:23; 11:2.
[123] 6:68; 9:38; 11:3, 12, 21, 27, 32, 34, 39; 13:6, 9, 25, 36, 37; 14:5, 8.
[124] 13:13, 14.   [125] John 6:69.   [126] See above, pp. 61–62.
[127] Mk. 7:19; 13:14.

The same distinction is made in regard to Christology. C. F. D. Moule long ago pointed out that Luke does not bring back into his first volume the Christology of the second.[128] Further extensive analysis has confirmed that Mark and Matthew are also careful to present Jesus in terms of the perceptual limits of people in the pre-Easter situation.[129] Jesus' own teaching was predominantly theocentric or, more precisely, 'patricentric'.[130] Although Jesus rather obliquely speaks of the 'Father' of the Son of man (implying that he is that Father's 'Son'), and of himself as 'beloved son' or 'the son', he does not directly refer to himself by the full-blown Christological titles 'Lord', 'Christ' or 'Son of God'. Nevertheless, while the 'then and there' distinction was preserved, it must be recognized that the authors wrote from the perspective of faith. Mark and Luke introduce Jesus to the reader in their opening pages as 'the Son of God', and Matthew introduces him immediately as 'the Christ'.

Like John, Matthew, Mark and Luke each have a developed Christology, but they do not put that Christology into the mouths of people in the pre-Easter situation. Moreover, that pre-Easter situation is portrayed in terms of the geography of that world and the politics of those times; not of elsewhere and later, but there and then.

The very genre chosen by the four writers, the *bios Iēsou*, the 'biography of Jesus', indicates, as R. Kysar has noted with respect to the gospel of John, 'that there is a real human life at the root of the central character of the witness. If flesh is irrelevant to the evangelist or if the revealer in no sense really took upon himself fleshly existence, why did the evangelist write a *gospel*?'[131]

Conclusion

In summary, my argument is that the gospel message was spread, and churches were established, by means of various mission teams associated with leaders such as James, Peter, John and Paul. Their chosen mode of addressing the issues in the

[128] C. F. D. Moule, 'The Christology of Acts', in *Studies in Luke-Acts*, ed. L. E. Keck and J. L. Martyn (New York: Abingdon, 1966), pp. 247–263.

[129] This is the thesis of E. E. Lemcio, *The Past of Jesus in the Gospels*.

[130] So Lemcio, *ibid.*, p. 113.

[131] R. Kysar, *The Fourth Evangelist and his Gospel* (Minneapolis: Augsburg, 1978), p. 191.

churches was a range of letters. From the 50s, when they began to appear, these letters apply the apostolic tradition to the wide range of problems which were by then impacting upon the churches.

Throughout the years of apostolic ministry, oral and written accounts of Jesus' teaching and deeds were being collected. The ethos of the early church was rabbinic, as developed out of the Judaism of that time. The four gospels represent the end point of the process of collecting traditional material which went back to Jesus. The four evangelists shaped the material which they had received into the four gospels. These have a more limited focus than the letters, that is, to provide *bioi*, biographies, of Jesus. As such the gospels belong to a recognized genre of the times. Although the gospels call for a faith-response to Jesus, they do so as authentically historical and biographical works which belong to their times.

Though perhaps (but by no means certainly) written a little later than (say) Paul's letters, the gospels address a more defined and confined subject, namely Jesus in his world and in his times, and in historically credible terms which he used of himself and which others used of him. That they do so is evidence of the impact Jesus the Teacher had on their living contemporaries, who had been with him. Yet the Jesus the readers meet in the gospels is a genuinely historical figure; he is Jesus 'back there'. The gospel writers are not cut off from Jesus. John and Matthew appear to have been original disciples; Mark and Luke wrote their gospels in dependence on those who were original disciples.

Gospel-writing was the end of a process of 'receiving' traditions, a Jewish activity arising within a Jewish ethos. The tradition reaches its final form through the creativity of the writers. But it is a creativity circumscribed by the received body of tradition as well as by the preached message of the apostles, who were interested in the historical circumstances of Jesus. This explains the phenomenon of the gospels, and accounts for their very biographical form and their interest in what Jesus said and did.

Chapter Eight

Jesus' death: a defiance of biography

My argument throughout has been that the fact of the early church, its 'faith' and 'proclamation', which are attested gratuitously in sources (the letters) close in time to Jesus, demands congruity between that 'faith' and 'proclamation' and his own person. In my view, the onlookers from the Roman world of the time understood this logical connection. It was precisely this link between the 'Christ' and the 'Christians' which was so unacceptable to them. He was 'another king', an alternative to their Caesar, and, in the eyes of the Christians, superior to Caesar. To the Romans these were 'messiah-people' a society-hating *superstitio*.

The four gospels, when they came to be written, were set in the style of the *bios* (biography) of that general era. Those gospels have in common, whatever else each sought to achieve, the intention to supply a *bios* of the one who had been proclaimed and who was the object of the churches' 'faith'. In this regard, as Burridge has argued, the gospels are identifiably *bioi*.[1] There is at least one point, however, in which the gospels as *bioi Iēsou* (biographies of Jesus) defy the pattern. In the place they give to his death and the space devoted to it, the gospels are at odds with the *bioi* of the times. Kähler's comment, that the gospels are passion narratives with an introduction, though overstated, expresses a brilliant insight.

To be sure, the biographies of the era frequently speak of the deaths of their subjects. Indeed, as Burridge as shown, the pattern of the last words, death and funeral of great men found across the *bioi*, to which the gospels also conform, is a reason to classify the gospels within this genre.[2] Suetonius usually has

---

[1] R. A. Burridge, *What are the Gospels?* (Cambridge: Cambridge University Press, 1995).

[2] *Ibid.*, pp. 208–209 (*cf.* p. 232). Burridge points out that the accounts of the

memorable details of the deaths of the Caesars and their 'famous last words', to take one example. Neither is the space devoted to the death of Jesus without parallel: a tenth of the *Agricola*, a sixth of *Cato Minor* and a quarter of *Apollonius of Tyana* are devoted to the death of the great man.[3]

How then does the gospels' interest in the death of Jesus defy the pattern found in contemporary *bioi*? First, the death of Jesus is intrinsic to the account of his life. Death hangs like a cloud over each narrative, from its beginning or near it.[4] The final journey to Jerusalem as narrated by Mark and Luke is a journey to rejection and death. Unlike the *bioi* of others, in the gospels Jesus' death is his true destiny and the inevitable outcome of his life. He lived in order to die.

Secondly, the death of Jesus was by means of an unmentionable mode of execution, namely crucifixion. In the unfolding of Christian history the cross has become a theological catchphrase as well as a visual symbol of Christianity. But within the immediacy of the event of Jesus' crucifixion, the impaling of victims was the ultimate and monstrous deterrent ('that most cruel and disgusting penalty')[5] used to restrain the lower orders within the empire.[6] Cicero stated that 'the very word "cross" should be far removed not only from the person of a Roman citizen but from his thoughts, his eyes and his ears'.[7] Yet none of the four gospels attempts to disguise the vile mode of Jesus' death. Strikingly, a *Roman* centurion, 'who stood facing him' at the foot of the execution pole, pronounced Jesus to be 'the Son of God'.[8]

Thirdly, the place given throughout the gospels to Jesus' death, and the space devoted to narrating it, are quite consistent with the proclamation of the apostles. This is explicit and frequent in the letters of Paul ('O . . . Galatians . . . before whose eyes Jesus Christ was publicly portrayed as *crucified*'; 'I decided to know nothing among you [Corinthians] except Jesus

---

deaths of certain men were used, first, to highlight the injustice of tyrants (p. 77), and secondly, to portray the real personalities of the subjects and to justify them morally (pp. 165–166).

[3] *Ibid.*, p. 167.   [4] Mt. 1:21; Mk. 3:5–6; Lk. 2:35; Jn. 1:29.

[5] Cicero, *Verres* 2.5.165.

[6] This is the thesis of M. Hengel, *Crucifixion* (London: SCM, 1977), pp. 33–45.

[7] *Pro Rabiro* 9–17.   [8] Mk. 15:39.

Christ . . . *crucified*').[9] Though not so clear in other New Testament writings, it is by no means absent.[10] The proclamation of Jesus' death, and that by *crucifixion*, was utterly without parallel in the Graeco-Roman world of that era, and, indeed, quite ridiculous in its eyes.[11]

To the Graeco-Romans of those times the message about Christ must have been quite bizarre. They understood well (too well!) that Christ was 'another king' and that Christians worshipped him as (a) god,[12] but a king or god whose *raison d'être* was death, and that by crucifixion! A graphic illustration of the stupidity of this in their eyes is the well-known third-century graffito from the Palatine Hill. A youth is worshipping a crucified man with an ass's head. The crudely written caption reads, 'Alexamenos worships his god.'[13] What utter folly: a god who is an ass – crucified!

The Jesus-studies movement, to generalize, has failed completely to account for the emphasis on Jesus' death as found consistently in both the gospels and the echoes of the proclamation about Jesus in the letters. To them, the death of Jesus is peripheral, whereas in the minds of the writers of the New Testament it was central. Why was it central? The most plausible answer is that it was central in the thinking of Jesus, which he in turn communicated to his core followers, who in turn diffused that belief throughout the earliest Christian traditions and from there into the pages of the literature as we have it. Jesus did not die as a martyr, but as one who knowingly died redemptively, for the sins of others, to set people free.[14]

[9] Gal. 3:1; 1 Cor. 2:2.   [10] Heb. 12:2; 1 Pet. 2:24; Rev. 11:8.

[11] 1 Cor. 1:23.   [12] So Pliny, *Epistle* x.96.7.

[13] Reproduced in Michael Green, *Evangelism in the Early Church* (London: Hodder and Stoughton, 1970), p. 174. M. Hengel, *Studies in Early Christology* (Edinburgh: T. and T. Clark, 1995), pp. 360–365.

[14] P. M. Head, 'The Self-Offering and Death of Christ as a Sacrifice in the Gospels and the Acts of the Apostles', in *Sacrifice in the Bible*, ed. R. T. Beckwith and M. J. Selman (Grand Rapids: Baker, 1995), pp. 112–129.

Chapter Nine

Conclusion

1. The practice of history is concerned with events and people and with change from one state to another. History is not concerned with 'things that are'. All primary sources must be surveyed, classified and evaluated. A helpful distinction may be made between self-consciously written history and information which may be inferred incidentally, gratuitously. The gospels and Acts belong to the former, while the letters provide the latter. Historical information found in the letters is of particular importance to the argument of this book.

2. The flood of literature attempting to recover the 'historical' Jesus has limited its field of enquiry to the Jesus of the gospels; the letters and the early church have generally been ignored. Yet the gospels have been used only in a selective manner, with much interest devoted to various proposed contexts for Jesus. In consequence, there is a bewildering list of idiosyncratic Jesuses who now confront us from numerous books, ranging from the esoterically academic to the fantastically bizarre. Some methodological controls are needed.

3. A review of Roman reactions to Jesus indicates great concern about an anti-Roman sect (a *superstitio*) generated by a certain *Christus*. Romans thought the Christians were proclaiming and worshipping 'another king' as superior to their emperor. By contrast, the Jesus of much modern scholarship terminates with himself, is movement-less, and makes no impact. Indeed, he is generally an unremarkable figure, unable to catapult any movement into motion.

4. The letters of Paul, James, Hebrews and 1 Peter reveal a proclamation of Christ, together with gratuitous reference to various biographical details about Jesus. The Christ of proclamation is anchored to the Jesus of history. The proclamation of Christ would have raised questions of the apostles by their hearers, eliciting various items of biographical information

about Jesus. The letter-writers can appeal to this information for pastoral purposes in such a way as to suggest that the readers only need the matter to be raised, however briefly, and they will know to what the writer is referring.

5. The best context in which to locate Jesus is discovered by text-based historical enquiry; sociological analysis, though useful, has significant limitations at this distance. The 'markers' of Luke 3:1–2 – John the baptizer, Herod the tetrarch, Annas and Caiaphas the high priests and Pontius Pilate the prefect – form an encircling context for Jesus. Yet Jesus is connected with each of these; they are not merely part of the landscape background. The Jesus of the gospels is tied into his various contexts, whether Galilean or Judean.

6. Because the gospels are self-consciously historical, a better way to begin to investigate Jesus is with the gratuitous information found in the letters. From these a rough grid may be established by which to validate or otherwise the gospels' accounts. The Jesus of the letters, who dies for sins, who is conscious that he is 'son' of *abba*, who prays and who seeks in Scripture the prophecies which he is fulfilling, gives strong affirmation of the integrity of the gospels. Some statements about the duration and broad shape of Jesus' method and ministry are possible, even if it is not possible to recover the 'real' Jesus.

7. The period in which the gospels were in process of formation is not unknown. We are able to discern a number of 'apostolates', reaching Jews on the one hand and Gentiles on the other. Their leaders kept in touch with their networks of churches through envoys and letters. Although a furious debate raged throughout the 50s over the basis on which Gentiles could be grafted into the people of God, involving the apostolic leaders James, Peter and Paul, there is little evidence of this as a concern of the gospels.

8. Two factors are helpful in understanding the origin of the gospels: first, the 'rabbinic' religious and educational culture of Jesus and early Christianity as a vehicle to pass on as well as to treasure the teachings of the Teacher; and secondly, the recognizably *bios* genre employed to tell about Jesus 'back there'. The letters have very wide interests, but the gospels a quite narrow interest. They are Jesus *bioi*. Their formation in a 'rabbinic' milieu by those who had not lost touch with Jesus, and

their final presentation in a *bios* format, contribute to our sense that they are historical documents.

9. Yet the dominant place of the death of Jesus, a death by the unmentionably vile mode of crucifixion, makes the *bios* or 'life' of Jesus distinct from any other *bios* of that era.

Bibliography

Alexander, P. S., 'Orality in Pharisaic-Rabbinic Judaism at the Turn of the Eras', in *Jesus and the Oral Gospel Tradition*, ed. H. Wansbrough (Sheffield: JSOT, 1991), pp. 159–184.

Allison, D. C., 'The Pauline Epistles and the Synoptic Gospels: The Patterns of the Parallels', *NTS* 28 (1982), pp. 1–32.

Barnett, P. W., 'Under Tiberius All was Quiet', *NTS* 21 (1975), pp. 564–571.

————'Who were the BIASTAI'? *RTR* xxxvi.3 (1977), pp. 67–70.

————'The Jewish Sign Prophets – AD 40–70: Their Intentions and Origin', *NTS* 27 (1980–81), pp. 279–297.

————'Opposition in Corinth', *JSNT* 22 (1984), pp. 3–17.

————*Is the New Testament History?* (London: Hodder and Stoughton, 1984).

————'The Feeding of the Multitude in Mark 6/John 6', *Gospel Perspectives* 6, ed. D. Wenham and C. Blomberg (Sheffield: JSOT, 1986), pp. 273–293.

————*The Two Faces of Jesus* (London: Hodder and Stoughton, 1990).

————*The Truth about Jesus* (Sydney: Aquila, 1994).

Barr, J., 'Abba Isn't "Daddy" ', *JTS* 39 (1988), pp. 28–47.

Barrett, C. K., *New Testament Background: Selected Documents* (New York: Harper and Row, 1987).

————*The Acts of the Apostles* 1 (Edinburgh: T. and T. Clark, 1994).

Bauckham, R., *Jude and the Relatives of Jesus in the Early Church* (Edinburgh: T. and T. Clark, 1990).

Baumgarten, A. I., 'Literary Evidence for Jewish Christianity', in *The Galilee of Late Antiquity*, ed. L. I. Levine (Cambridge, MA: Harvard University Press, 1992).

Beker, J. C., 'Contingency and Coherence in the Letters of Paul', *USQR* XXXIII (1978), pp. 141–151.

Belleville, L., 'Gospel and Kerygma', in *Gospel and Paul*, ed. L. A. Jervis and P. Richardson (Sheffield: JSOT, 1994), pp. 137–140.

Best, E., '1 Peter and the Gospel Tradition', *NTS* 16 (1969), pp. 95–113.

Bockmuehl, M., *This Jesus: Martyr, Lord, Messiah* (Edinburgh: T. and T. Clark, 1994).

Borg, M., *Jesus: A New Vision* (San Francisco: Harper and Row, 1988).

————'A Renaissance in Jesus Studies', *ThT* 45 (1988), pp. 280–292.

Brandon, S. G. F., *Jesus and the Zealots* (Manchester: Manchester University Press, 1967).

Brown, R. E., *The Gospel According to John* (London: Chapman, 1966).

Bruce, F. F., 'Christianity under Claudius', *BJRL* 44 (1962), pp. 315–318.

————*New Testament History* (London: Oliphants, 1969).

————*Jesus and Christian Origins outside the New Testament* (Grand Rapids: Eerdmans, 1974).

————*Commentary on Galatians* (Exeter: Paternoster, 1982).

Burridge, R. A., *What are the Gospels?* (Cambridge: Cambridge University Press, 1992).

Caragounis, C., *The Son of Man* (Tübingen: Mohr, 1986).

Carr, E. H., *What is History?* (Harmondsworth: Penguin, 1961).

Carson, D. A., 'Understanding Misunderstandings in the Fourth Gospel', *TB* 33 (1982), pp. 58–89.

————'The Purpose of the Fourth Gospel: John 20:31 Reconsidered', *JBL* 108 (1987), pp. 639–651.

————'Redaction Criticism', in *Scripture and Truth*, ed. D. A. Carson and J. D. Woodbridge (Grand Rapids: Baker, rev. edn. 1995).

————'Do the Prophets and the Law Quit Prophesying Before John? A Note on Matthew 11:13', in *The Gospels and the Scriptures of Israel*, ed. C. A. Evans and W. R. Stegner, *JSNT* Supplement Series 104 (Sheffield: Sheffield Academic Press, 1995), pp. 179–194.

Chilton, B., *Profiles of a Rabbi* (Atlanta: Scholars, 1989).

Crossan, J. D., *The Historical Jesus: The Life of a Mediterranean Jewish Peasant* (San Francisco: Harper, 1991).

Crown, A. D., and Cansdale, L., 'Qumran: Was it an Essene Settlement?' *BAR* 20/5 (1994), pp. 25ff.

Davies, P. S., 'The Meaning of Philo's Text about the Gilded Shields', *JTS* 37 (1986), pp. 109–114.

Dodd, C. H., *Historical Tradition in the Fourth Gospel* (Cambridge: Cambridge University Press, 1963).

Dunn, J. D. G., *Unity and Diversity in the New Testament* (London: SCM, 1977).

————'The Relationship Between Paul and Jerusalem According to Gal i and ii', in *Jesus, Paul and the Law: Studies in Mark and Galatians* (London: SPCK, 1990).

————'John and the Oral Tradition', in *Jesus and the Oral Gospel Tradition*, ed. H. Wansbrough (Sheffield: JSOT, 1991), pp. 351–379.

————'Jesus Tradition in Paul', in *Studying the Historical Jesus*, ed. B. Chilton and C. Evans (Leiden: Brill, 1994), pp. 155–178.

Edwards, D., 'The Socio-Economic and Cultural Ethos of the Lower Galilee in the First Century: Implications for the Nascent Jesus Movement in the Galilee', in *The Galilee of Late Antiquity*, ed. L. I. Levine (Cambridge, MA: Harvard University Press, 1992), pp. 53–73.

Ellis, E. E., 'Dating the New Testament', *NTS* 26 (1980), pp. 487–488.

————'The Date and Provenance of Mark's Gospel', in *The Four Gospels 1992*, II, ed. F. Van Segbroeck (Leuven: Leuven University Press, 1992), pp. 801–815.

Elton, G. R., *The Practice of History* (Sydney: Sydney University Press, 1967).

Evans, C. A., *Jesus* (Grand Rapids: Baker, 1992).

————'Jesus in Non-Christian Sources', in *Studying the Historical Jesus*, ed. B. Chilton and C. A. Evans (Leiden: Brill, 1994), pp. 443–478.

Farmer, W. R., *The Gospel of Jesus: The Pastoral Relevance of the Synoptic Problem* (Louisville: Westminster John Knox, 1994).

Ferguson, L., 'Canon Muratori: Date and Provenance', *SP* XVII.2 (1982), pp. 677–683.

Foster, J., *After the Apostles* (London: SCM, 1961).

France, R. T., *Jesus and the Old Testament* (London: Tyndale, 1971).

————'Jesus the Baptist?' in *Jesus of Nazareth: Lord and Christ*, ed. J. B. Green and M. Turner (Grand Rapids: Eerdmans, 1994), pp. 94–111.

Freyne, S., *Galilee from Alexander the Great to Hadrian: A Study of Second-Temple Judaism* (Wilmington: Glazier, 1980).

————'Urban–Rural Relationships in First-Century Galilee: Some Suggestions from the Literary Sources', in *The Galilee of*

Late Antiquity, ed. L. I. Levine (Cambridge, MA: Harvard University Press, 1992), pp. 75–91.

————'The Geography, Politics and Economics of Galilee', in *Studying the Historical Jesus*, ed. B. Chilton and C. A. Evans (Leiden: Brill, 1994), pp. 75–121.

Gardner-Smith, P., *Saint John and the Synoptic Gospels* (Cambridge: Cambridge University Press, 1938).

Gerhardsson, B., *Memory and Manuscript* (Uppsala: Lund, 1964).

————'The Narrative Meshalim in the Synoptic Gospels', *NTS* 34 (1988), pp. 339–363.

Green, M., *Evangelism in the Early Church* (London: Hodder and Stoughton, 1970).

Gundry, R. H., '*Verba Christi* in 1 Peter: Their Implications Concerning the Authorship of 1 Peter and the Authenticity of the Gospel Tradition', *NTS* 13 (1966), pp. 336–350.

————'Further Verb on *Verba Christi* in 1 Peter', *Bib* 55 (1974), pp. 211–232.

Guthrie, D. G., *New Testament Introduction* (Leicester: Apollos, 4th edn. 1990).

Harrington, D. J., 'The Jewishness of Jesus: Facing Some Problems', *CBQ* 49 (1987), pp. 1–13.

Hartin, J., *James and the Q Sayings of Jesus* (Sheffield: JSOT, 1991).

Hatina, T., 'Jewish Religious Backgrounds of the New Testament', in *Approaches to New Testament Study*, ed. S. Porter (Sheffield: JSOT, 1995), pp. 48–49.

Head, P. M., 'The Self-Offering and Death of Christ as a Sacrifice in the Gospels and the Acts of the Apostles', in *Sacrifice in the Bible*, ed. R. T. Beckwith and M. J. Selman (Grand Rapids: Baker, 1995), pp. 112–129.

Hebblethwaite, B., 'The Jewishness of Jesus from the Perspectives of Christian Doctrine', *SJT* 42 (1989), pp. 27–44.

Hemer, C. J., *The Book of Acts in the Setting of Hellenistic History* (Tübingen: Mohr, 1989).

Hengel, M., *The Son of God* (London: SCM, 1976).

————*Crucifixion* (London: SCM, 1977).

————*Acts and the History of Earliest Christianity* (London: SCM, 1979).

————*Between Jesus and Paul* (London: SCM, 1983).

————*Studies in the Gospel of Mark* (London: SCM, 1985).

————*The 'Hellenization' of Judaea in the First Century After Christ* (London: SCM, 1989).

————*The Pre-Christian Paul* (London: SCM, 1991).

————*Studies in Early Christology* (Edinburgh: T. and T. Clark, 1995).

Hoehner, H., *Chronological Aspects of the Life of Christ* (Grand Rapids: Zondervan, 1977).

————*Herod Antipas* (Grand Rapids: Zondervan, 1980).

Horsley, R. A., *Galilee* (Valley Forge: Trinity, 1995).

————and Hanson, J. S., *Bandits, Prophets and Messiahs* (Minneapolis: Winston, 1985).

Humphreys, C. J., and Waddington, W. G., 'Astronomy and the Date of the Crucifixion', in *Chronos, Kairos, Christos*, ed. J. Vardaman and E. M. Yamauchi (Winona Lake: Eisenbrauns, 1989), pp.165–181.

Jeremias, J., 'The Key to Pauline Theology', *ExpT* 76 (1964–5), pp. 27–32.

Judge, E. A., and Thomas, G. S. R., 'The Origin of the Church at Rome', *RTR* xxv (1966), pp. 81–92.

Kähler, M., *The So-Called Historical Jesus and the Historic Biblical Christ* (Philadelphia: Fortress, 1964).

Keck, L. E., *A Future for the Historical Jesus* (Nashville: Abingdon, 1971).

Kelber, W., *The Oral and Written Gospel: The Hermeneutics of Speaking and Writing in the Synoptic Tradition, Mark, Paul and Q* (Philadelphia: Fortress, 1983).

Kelly, J. N. D., *The Epistles of Peter and Jude* (London: A. and C. Black, 1969).

Kümmel, W. G., *Introduction to the New Testament* (London: SCM, 1975).

Kysar, R., *The Fourth Evangelist and his Gospel* (Minneapolis: Augsburg, 1978).

————'The Contribution of D. Moody-Smith to Johannine Scholarship', in *Exploring the Gospel of John*, ed. R. A. Culpepper and C. C. Black (Louisville: Westminister, 1996), pp. 3–17.

Ladd, G. E., *The Presence of the Future* (Grand Rapids: Eerdmans, 1974).

Lemcio, E. E., *The Past of Jesus in the Gospels* (Cambridge: Cambridge University Press, 1991).

Levine, L. I. (ed.), *The Galilee of Late Antiquity* (Cambridge, MA: Harvard University Press, 1992).

Linnemann, E., 'The Lost Gospel of Q – Fact or Fantasy?' *TJ* 17 (1966), pp. 3–18.

McDonald, L. M., 'The Integrity of the Biblical Canon in Light of its Historical Development', *BBR* 6 (1996), pp. 95–132.

McGing, B., 'Pontius Pilate and the Sources', *CBQ* 53/3 (1991), pp. 416–438.

McLaren, J. S., *Power and Politics in Palestine: The Jews and the Governing of their Land 100 BC–AD 70*, *JSOT* Supplement Series 63 (Sheffield: JSOT, 1991).

Maier, P. L., 'Sejanus, Pilate and the Date of the Crucifixion', *CH* xxxvii (1969), pp. 3–13.

————'The Episode of the Golden Roman Shields in Jerusalem', *HTR* lxii (1969), pp. 109–121.

————'The Date of the Nativity and the Chronology of Jesus' Life', in *Chronos, Kairos, Christos*, ed. J. Vardaman and E. M. Yamauchi (Winona Lake: Eisenbrauns, 1989), pp. 113–130.

Malina, B., *The New Testament World: Insights from Cultural Anthropology* (Louisville: Westminster John Knox, 1993).

Manson, T. W., *The Servant Messiah* (Cambridge: Cambridge University Press, 1961).

Mayor, J. B., *The Epistle of James* (London: Macmillan, 1913).

Meier, J. P., *A Marginal Jew: Rethinking the Historical Jesus* 1 (New York: Doubleday, 1991).

Meyer, B. F., *The Aims of Jesus* (London: SCM, 1979).

Meyers, E. F., and Strange, J. F., *Archaeology, the Rabbis and Early Christianity* (London: SCM, 1981).

Montefiore, H. W., 'Revolt in the Desert?', *NTS* 8 (1962), pp. 135–141.

Moule, C. F. D., 'The Christology of Acts', in *Studies in Luke-Acts*, ed. L. E. Keck and J. L. Martyn (New York: Abingdon, 1966), pp. 247–263.

————*The Phenomenon of the New Testament* (London: SCM, 1967).

————*The Origin of Christology* (Cambridge: Cambridge University Press, 1978).

Murphy-O'Connor, J., *St Paul's Corinth* (Wilmington: Glazier, 1983).

Patterson, S., 'Q the Lost Gospel', *BR* IX/5 (October 1993), pp. 35ff.

Reif, S. C., *Judaism and Hebrew Prayer* (Cambridge: Cambridge University Press, 1993).

Ridderbos, H. N., *Paul and Jesus* (Nutley: Presbyterian and Reformed, 1977).

Riesner, R., 'Bethany Beyond the Jordan (John 1:28): Topography, Theology and History in the Fourth Gospel', *TB* 38 (1987), pp. 29–63.

————'Jesus as Preacher and Teacher', in *Jesus and the Oral Gospel Tradition*, ed. H. Wansbrough (Sheffield: JSOT, 1991), pp. 185–210.

Robinson, J. A. T., *Redating the New Testament* (London: SCM, 1976).

————*The Priority of John* (London: SCM, 1985).

Saldarini, A. J., 'The Gospel of Matthew and Jewish–Christian Conflict', in *The Galilee of Late Antiquity*, ed. L. I. Levine (Cambridge, MA: Harvard University Press, 1992), pp. 23–38.

Sanders, E. P., *Jesus and Judaism* (London: SCM, 1984).

Schürer, E., *The History of the Jewish People in the Age of Jesus Christ* (Edinburgh: T. and T. Clark, rev. edn. 1979).

Sherwin-White, A. N., *Roman Society and Roman Law in the New Testament* (Oxford: Oxford University Press, 1963).

Slingerland, D., 'Suetonius Claudius 25.4 and the Account in Dio Cassius', *JQR* 79 (1989), pp. 305–322.

Smallwood, E. M., 'Some Notes on the Jews under Tiberius', *Latomus* xv (1956), pp. 109–121.

————'Philo and Josephus as Historians of the Same Event', in *Josephus, Judaism and Christianity*, ed. L. H. Feldman and G. Hata (Leiden: Brill, 1986), pp. 114–129.

Soards, M. L., 'Tradition, Composition and Theology in Luke's Account of Jesus', *Bib* 66/3 (1985), pp. 344–363.

Stanton, G. N., *Jesus of Nazareth in New Testament Preaching*, SNTS Monograph Series 27 (Cambridge: Cambridge University Press, 1974).

————*The Gospels and Jesus* (Oxford: Oxford University Press, 1989).

Tasker, R. V. G., 'St Paul and the Earthly Life of Jesus', *ExpT* 46 (1934–5), pp. 557–62.

Telford, W. R., 'Major Trends and Interpretative Issues in the Study of Jesus', in *Studying the Historical Jesus*, ed. B. Chilton and C. A. Evans (Leiden: Brill, 1994), pp. 33–74.

Theissen, G., *The Gospels in Context: Social and Political History in the Synoptic Tradition* (Edinburgh: T. and T. Clark, 1992).

Thompson, M., *Clothed with Christ: The Example and Teaching of Jesus in Rom 12.1 – 15.13*, *JSNT* Supplement Series 59 (Sheffield: JSOT, 1991).

Thompson, M. M., 'The Historical Jesus and the Johannine Jesus', in *Exploring the Gospel of John*, ed. R. A. Culpepper and C. C. Black (Louisville: Westminister John Knox, 1996), pp. 21–42.

Tuni, J. O., 'Jesus of Nazareth in the Christology of 1 Peter', *HJ* xxviii/3 (1987), pp. 292–304.

Webb, R. L., 'John the Baptist and his Relationship with Jesus', in *Studying the Historical Jesus*, ed. B. Chilton and C. A. Evans (Leiden: Brill, 1994), pp. 179–229.

Wedderburn, A. J. M., 'Paul and Jesus: The Problem of Continuity', *SJT* 38 (1985), pp. 202–203.

————'Paul and the Story of Jesus', in *Paul and Jesus* (Sheffield: JSOT, 1989), pp. 161–189.

Wenham, D., 'The Story of Jesus Known to Paul', in *Jesus of Nazareth: Lord and Christ*, ed. J. B. Green and M. Turner (Grand Rapids: Eerdmans, 1994), pp. 297–311.

————*Paul: Follower of Jesus or Founder of Christianity?* (Grand Rapids: Eerdmans, 1995).

Wilcox, M., 'Jesus in the Light of His Jewish Environment', *ANRW* ii (1982), pp. 131–195.

Wilken, R., *Christians as the Romans Saw Them* (New Haven: Yale University Press, 1984).

Wilkins, J., and Moreland, P. (eds.), *Jesus Under Fire* (Grand Rapids: Zondervan, 1995).

Winter, B. W. (series editor), *The Book of Acts in its First-Century Setting*, 6 vols. (Grand Rapids: Eerdmans, 1993–).

Witherington, B., *The Christology of Jesus* (Minneapolis: Fortress, 1990).

————*Jesus the Sage* (Edinburgh: T. and T. Clark, 1994).

————*The Jesus Quest* (Downers Grove: IVP, 1995).

Wright, N. T., 'Quest for the Historical Jesus', *Anchor Bible Dictionary* 3 (Garden City, NY: Doubleday, 1992), pp. 796–802.

Index of authors

Index of Bible references

Deuteronomy
21:3, *94*

2 Samuel
7:8–16, *97*

Psalms
2:1–12, *97*

Isaiah
11:1, *97*
53:4, *99*
53:5, *99*
53:6, *99*
53:10, *99*
53:12, *99*

Micah
5:1–3, *97*

Haggai
2:20–23, *97*

Zechariah
9:9, *97*

Matthew
1:16, *58*
1:21, *160*
3:1–10, *64*
3:1–12, *65*
3:2, *107*
4:12–13, *65*
4:15–17, *150*
4:24–25, *151*
5:17–19, *154*

5:18, *154*
5:19, *51*
5:25–26, *73*
5:34–37, *51*
6:14, *23*
7:1, *51*
7:3–5, *44*
7:8–9, *44*
7:11, *51*
7:13, *44*
7:24, *69*
8:5–13, *72*
9:9, *150*
10:3, *150*
10:5–6, *150*
11:3, *23*
11:7–8, *77*
11:10, *23*
11:28–30, *109, 139*
11:29, *58*
12:36, *51*
14:1, *69*
14:9, *69*
14:13, *74, 76*
15:11, *51*
15:21–24, *150*
16:13–20, *151*
17:24–27, *73*
18:11, *51*
20:1–16, *87*
25:3, *51*
27:37, *82*
28:1–6, *130*
28:11–15, *130*
28:16–20, *151*
28:19, *150*

28:19–20, *142*

Mark
1:9–11, *113*
1:14, *65*
1:14–15, *107, 113*
1:16–20, *139*
1:21, *108*
1:39, *108*
2:6, *107*
2:14–17, *150*
2:23, *113*
3:5–6, *160*
3:6, *71*
3:21, *107*
3:22, *74, 107*
4:10–12, *108*
4:10–20, *108*
4:33–34, *108*
5:1, *61*
6:4, *110*
6:10, *112*
6:14, *69, 75*
6:14–15, *107*
6:30–44, *104*
6:30–45, *113*
6:39, *113*
7:1, *74*
7:3, *138*
7:17–23, *108*
7:24, *61*
7:39, *156*
8:26–27, *61*
8:28, *107*
8:29, *77*
9:28–29, *108*